SCIENTIFIC
AMERICAN **SOURCEBOOKS**

# THE SOLAR SYSTEM
## FACTS AND EXPLORATION

**GREGORY L. VOGT**

**TWENTY-FIRST CENTURY BOOKS**

*A Division of Henry Holt and Company*
*New York*

Twenty-First Century Books / A Division of Henry Holt and Company, Inc. / *Publishers since 1866*
115 West 18th Street / New York, NY 10011

**Library of Congress Cataloging-in-Publication Data**

Vogt, Gregory L. / The solar system : facts and exploration / Gregory L. Vogt. — 1st ed.
p. cm. — (Scientific American sourcebooks). Includes bibliographical references and index.
1. Outer space—Exploration—Juvenile literature. 2. Planets—Exploration—Juvenile literature.
3. Interplanetary voyages—Juvenile literature. [1. Solar system. 2. Outer space.] I. Title. II. Series.
QB500.22.V64 1995        523.2—dc20                                                    95–941

ISBN 0–8050–3249–5 (hardcover) / ISBN 0–8050–3248–7 (paperback)
First Edition 1995

*This book is dedicated to Professor Michael Sherman,*
*who kindled my interest in other worlds.*

# CONTENTS

# INTRODUCTION

OCTOBER 5, 1957    It was one of those days when the whole world changed forever. The event that triggered the change had taken place the day before, but few people knew about it. When the announcement was made, however, the whole world paid attention. The *New York Times*, like many newspapers around the globe, startled its readers with banner headlines: SOVIET FIRES EARTH SATELLITE INTO SPACE; IT IS CIRCLING THE GLOBE AT 18,000 M.P.H.; SPHERE TRACKED IN 4 CROSSINGS OVER U.S.

The Soviet Union described its satellite as a shiny metal sphere with four spikelike antennas. It weighed 184 pounds (83 kilograms) and was 22 inches (56 centimeters) in diameter. A powerful rocket carried the satellite into space and placed it in an orbit that reached as high as 560 miles (900 kilometers) above the Earth. Shooting through space at 18,000 miles (28,970 kilometers) per hour, the satellite was orbiting the Earth every ninety-five minutes, or fifteen times each day. Because Earth was rotating under the satellite as it orbited, each orbit crossed over a different part of the planet. Several times each day the Soviet satellite passed directly over the United States!

The launch of the world's first artificial satellite was an exciting event. But it was also frightening, because the Soviet Union was a bitter rival of the United States. Many people believed it was only a matter of time before the two nations would become locked in an atomic war that could end the world. Now, with the launch of the satellite, the possibility of atomic war seemed much closer. Scientists in the Soviet Union had done something that

**S**putnik 1

American scientists had yet to achieve. If the Soviets could launch a satellite, they could also use their rockets as missiles to propel atomic bombs right into the heart of the United States. Worse still, some people thought bombs could be placed in satellites and rain down from space with no warning!

Rather than signaling the end of civilization, the first satellite launch turned out to be the start of something wonderful. It was the beginning of the space age—a time in which machines and human beings would leave the surface of the Earth to become explorers of the solar system and beyond. Our knowledge of Earth's place in the universe would grow at an explosive rate.

Regardless of any military motives the Soviet Union had for launching a satellite, the world became a better place that day. In their written statement about the event, the Soviets called the satellite a "tremendous contribution to the treasure house of world science and culture" and said it would be used for "studying Earth as part of our solar system." They even gave the satellite a peaceful name. They called it *Sputnik*, a word that means "something that is traveling with a traveler." The "something" was the satellite, and the "traveler" was the Earth, voyaging through space in its orbit around the Sun.

Now, more than three decades after *Sputnik*'s launch, we know much about our planet and its place in the solar system. The satellites and the interplanetary spacecraft that followed *Sputnik* into outer space have enabled us to see our solar system in new ways. Telescopes on satellites orbiting above Earth's filtering atmosphere gained a clearer view of the distant planets than was possible with Earth-based telescopes. Rocket-propelled spacecraft shot by the cloud tops of distant planets, swung into planetary orbits, and dropped lander vehicles packed with scientific instruments to sample the atmosphere and soil of worlds very different from our own. Because of this, our knowledge of our solar system has multiplied many times over. To see how much things have changed, let us go back to 1950, to a time before spacecraft. What did we know about our solar system then?

**THE SOLAR SYSTEM AT THE DAWN OF THE SPACE AGE** By the 1950s scientists knew the solar system consisted of a central star, nine planets, more than thirty moons, and assorted comets, meteors, and asteroids. Our sun was known to be an average-sized star that released tremendous amounts of energy into space.

The innermost planet was Mercury, a rocky world that was cooked on the side nearest the Sun and frozen on the other. Since Mercury appeared as just a small bright spot in even the most powerful telescopes, scientists who study the objects in our solar system and the universe could only guess at what the planet might be like.

Though Venus, the second planet out from the Sun, was the same size as Earth and closest to us, it guarded its secrets carefully. A thick layer of white clouds shrouded the planet, preventing even the briefest peek at its surface. Still, scientists speculated about Venus. It would have to be a hot planet covered with oily seas or perhaps thick jungles.

Earth's nearest neighbor was its satellite, the Moon. Because of its closeness and lack of an atmosphere, scientists could study its near side in great detail. The Moon had many craters that could have been caused by the impacts of meteoroids, space rocks crashing into its surface, or by volcanic eruptions. There were also broad, dark plains that might be covered with thick layers of dust. The dust layers could be a quicksandlike hazard for any future space traveler who attempted to walk on the Moon's surface.

Mars, half again as far out from the Sun as Earth, was thought to be a good candidate for a planet harboring life. Through telescopes, scientists could see annual color changes in the planet's surface that might be caused by the seasonal growth of plants. Some scientists even thought they saw canals crisscrossing Mars's surface. Perhaps there were Martians on Mars who used the canals to transport meltwater from polar ice caps to the planet's drier equatorial regions. Mars was known to have two tiny moons.

Much farther away from the Sun was the giant planet Jupiter. Its surface was covered with reddish and white belts of clouds stretching around the planet. There was also a great oval-shaped red spot three times larger than Earth. Was it a storm or just the tops of some high mountains poking through the cloud belts? Four very large moons and eight small moons circled Jupiter. Scientists believed that Jupiter probably consisted mostly of gas surrounding a rocky inner core.

Farther out still was Saturn, another giant gas planet. Saturn was surrounded by three flat rings stretching thousands of miles out into space and had nine moons orbiting it.

Well beyond Saturn were the three most distant planets—Uranus, Neptune, and Pluto. Uranus looked greenish in Earth's telescopes and had five moons. Neptune was faintly bluish and had two moons. Pluto was merely a tiny white dot with no known moons circling it. Uranus and Neptune were also believed to be gas planets, while Pluto was thought to consist of rock and ice.

In the 1950s scientists knew or thought they knew much about our solar system. But with the dawn of the space age, even their most basic ideas would be challenged by the wealth of new data that spacecraft collected. What has been learned? What is our solar system really like? Let us explore our solar system via some of the spacecraft that have ventured into the vacuum of space. The home base for our explorations is our Earth. As we learn about strange new worlds, we will use Earth for comparison.

**PLUTO**

**NEPTUNE**

In this painting of the solar system,
only a small portion of our enormous
Sun is shown. Giant Jupiter is clearly
the largest of the nine planets, with
Saturn next in size. Venus and Earth
are very similar in size, and Pluto
shows as the tiniest planet of all.
Each of the planets, except Mercury
and Venus, has moons, but none of
them are shown here. Between
them, Jupiter and Saturn have a
total of thirty-four moons!

**EARTH**

**VENUS**

**MERCURY**

**PLUTO**

# ONE

# *THE SUN*
## CENTER OF GRAVITY AND LIGHT

Our exploration of the solar system will lead us to nine planets, an extensive system of moons, and many smaller bodies, including comets, asteroids, and meteors. The system is complex and in constant motion. The Sun, our central star, keeps the planets and all the other objects of our solar system from drifting off into space by providing gravity, a force that causes all objects to attract one another. The Sun is also the source of light that illuminates our solar system, so life can exist on Earth.

If we could leap out into very deep space, a million times farther than we are now, and could look back, we would see that our Sun is merely an average star. It would hardly be noticeable among the hundred or so billion stars that make up our Milky Way galaxy. Many stars are far bigger than our Sun, and many are far brighter.

Even though it is merely an average star, the Sun is nevertheless remarkable. It floods tremendous quantities of energy out into space—energy that we see as light. Here on Earth, 93 million miles (150 million kilometers) away, we receive only a tiny fraction of the Sun's energy release—about one-billionth of the total!

The Sun is a bright sphere of hydrogen and helium gases. The atoms in these gases are split into subatomic particles (electrons and protons) and rearranged into ions. Ions are atoms that have fewer or greater numbers of electrons orbiting their nuclei than normal. When ions have fewer electrons orbiting their nuclei, they are positively charged. When they have more, they are negatively charged. The driving force behind the rearrangement of

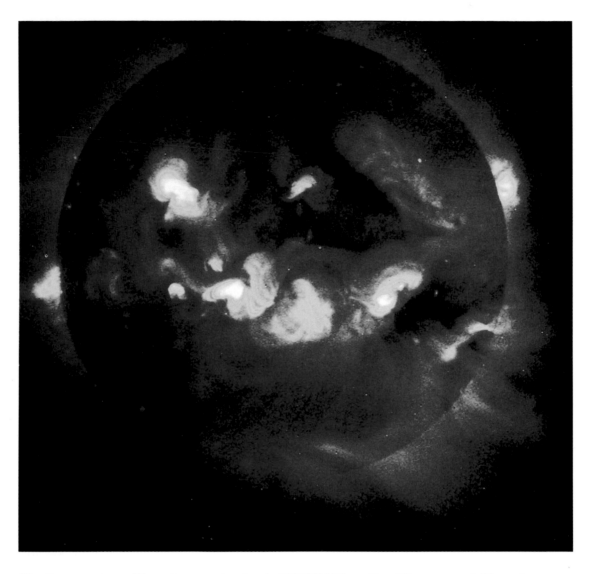

*The Sun, seen in an X-ray image taken by the YOHKOH satellite. X rays, not visible to the human eye, reveal the intense activity taking place in the sun's corona, the outer layer of the solar atmosphere.*

the Sun's gas atoms is the Sun's great temperature. Deep inside its core, the temperature climbs to as high as 16,000,000°F (8,900,000°C).

Part of the reason the Sun is so hot at its core is its great size and mass. The Sun is an enormous sphere 864,000 miles (1,390,000 kilometers) in diameter. If the Sun were hollow, it would take more than a million planet Earths to fill it. Another way to illustrate the Sun's great size is to imagine a necklace strung with Earth-sized beads. The necklace would require 345 beads just to circle the Sun. But because the Sun is made up of compressed gases, it is less dense than Earth, a planet that is made up mostly of rock and metal. If you could place the Sun on one side of a scale, you would need about 333,400 Earths on the other side of the scale just to balance it. In other words, if Earth were as large as the Sun, it would weigh three times more than the Sun because it is more densely packed.

An object the Sun's size exerts tremendous pressure on the atoms located at its core. With pressure comes high temperatures. But pressure alone could not generate temperatures as high as 16,000,000°F. Something else is happening inside the Sun.

To learn about this mystery and others, let's take an imaginary voyage inside the Sun. We will ride in a vehicle that is impervious to heat. Our dive into the Sun begins when we encounter its atmosphere. The atmosphere is a huge sphere surrounding the Sun. It is divided into two main parts. The outer part is the corona. We encounter the corona while we are still millions of miles from the Sun. But without sensitive scientific instruments, we would not know we were passing through it. The gases that make up the corona are so thin (the atoms are spread widely apart) that they are practically nonexistent. In the bright light of the Sun, the corona is invisible, too. You might be wondering how, if the corona is so thin and hard to see, we know it is there. The corona can be seen from Earth during a solar eclipse when the Sun is covered up by Earth's moon. Then the corona's faint light, no brighter than the light from the full Moon, becomes visible.

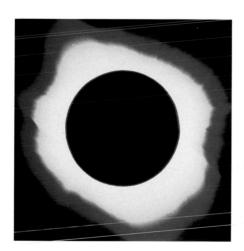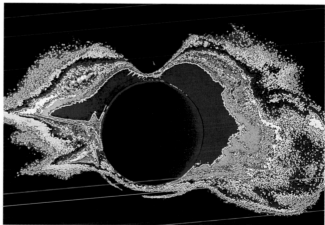

*T*wo views of the Sun's corona during a solar eclipse. The Sun's surface is out of sight behind Earth's moon in both pictures. The photograph on the right has been color enhanced to show different levels of heat in the corona.

## • HOW FAR? HOW BIG? HOW HOT? •

Scientists are very clever about the way they collect their scientific data. If they can hold an object in their hands, it is easy to know everything about it. But if the object is very far away, learning about it is more difficult. For example, how do we know the temperature on Mars? The answer involves the use of mathematics.

If you see two nearby objects at different distances from you, you can tell which one is farther away just by looking at them. You can do that because you have two eyes set apart from each other. Each eye sees the objects from a slightly different angle, and your brain interprets these differences as distance.

Scientists use a similar technique with the objects in our solar system. For example, if scientists in two distant cities each measure the angle of the Moon above the horizon, they will each get different angles. Using a form of mathematics known as trigonometry, they can calculate how far away the Moon is. They factor three things into their equations: the two angles they measured and the distance between the two cities. The distance between the cities can be determined by direct measurement. By solving their equation, the scientists obtain the distance to the Moon. The same technique can be used to determine the distance to the planets and the Sun.

There are lots of other ways of measuring distances in space. For example, if you measure how long it takes for radar waves to bounce off Venus and return to Earth, you can tell how far away Venus is. Radar waves travel at the speed of light (186,000 miles or 300,000 kilometers per second). The round-trip travel time in seconds divided by two is multiplied by the speed of light to get the distance.

Once you know how far away a planet is, you can determine how large it is by measuring how big it appears in the sky. Again, mathematics is used to arrive at an answer. Another thing you can learn about a planet is its temperature, by measuring the amount of energy it gives off in space. By knowing how far away the planet is, you can use mathematics to calculate the planet's temperature.

The corona often has large bulges and holes that reach downward almost to the Sun's surface.

The corona's temperature ranges from 1,000,000 to 5,000,000°F (555,282 to 2,778,000°C). Yet as we pass through the corona, we don't feel much heat. Remember, the atoms of gas in the corona are spread widely apart. Even though their temperature is high, they don't contain much heat. To understand this, think of an oven set at 400°F (204°C). You can reach into the oven without burning your hands because the air in the oven is thin and does not contain much heat. However, don't try to pick up a cake pan inside the oven without oven mitts! The cake pan is made of metal and is much denser than air. It contains a great deal of heat and will burn your hands if they are not protected.

About 1,600 miles (2,600 kilometers) from the Sun's surface, we pass into the inner atmosphere. This is the chromosphere. During an eclipse, scientists see the chromosphere as a ragged pink ring surrounding the Sun. Like the corona, the chromosphere barely exists because its atoms of gas, mostly hydrogen, are so far apart. However, temperatures in the chromosphere are much lower than those in the corona. Beginning at the corona-chromosphere boundary, temperatures drop from 1,000,000 to 9,540°F (555,282 to 5,282°C).

The chromosphere is constantly ripped open by storms from the Sun's surface. Called spicules because they are spike-shaped, these storms blast up thousands of miles into the corona. More powerful are flares that erupt from the Sun's surface. They are equivalent to the simultaneous explosion of ten million hydrogen bombs. The flares shoot long streams of electrically charged particles through the chromosphere and corona. Sometimes these streams reach all the way to Earth, where they interact with Earth's upper atmosphere to produce the northern and southern lights—aurora borealis and aurora australis—and disrupt radio communications.

Even greater than solar flares are the prominences, which are like huge moving curtains of glowing gas. Arching above the chromosphere, the gas in the prominences usually condenses out of the corona, like a hot rain, to fall into the Sun. But other prominences form as the result of huge explosions in the Sun's surface that shoot millions of tons of hot gas several hundred thousand of miles into the corona before falling back.

Dipping below the chromosphere, we reach the source of all this violence, the Sun's photosphere. This is the bright solar surface. Most of the light we see from the Sun comes from here. It is a layer of brightly glowing gas that extends into the Sun a few hundred miles. It is here, at the Sun's outer edge, that the Sun's temperature drops to only 6,460°F (3,571°C). The dropping temperature is one of the great mysteries of the Sun that scientists hope to solve someday. (The temperature should rise as we get closer to the Sun's surface.)

The photosphere seethes with boiling gases. If you look at the surface of a pot of simmering soup, you can see hot soup rising to the top in the middle, spreading out to the sides, and falling back to the bottom. It is the same with the gases in the photosphere. Large pools of hot gas boil up to the surface. Millions of these pools, called granules, crowd against one another. Along the edges where granules come together, spicules form and erupt up into the chromosphere and corona.

Sometimes spots of slightly cooler gas form on the photosphere. These sunspots, ranging from about 600 miles (965 kilometers) to tens of thousands of miles in diameter, are a few hundred degrees cooler than the rest of the photosphere. Because they are cooler, they appear dark compared to their surroundings. The presence of sunspots enabled scientists to learn that the Sun rotates on an axis. This discovery was made because sunspots can last many days or weeks before disappearing. Each day, scientists noted that

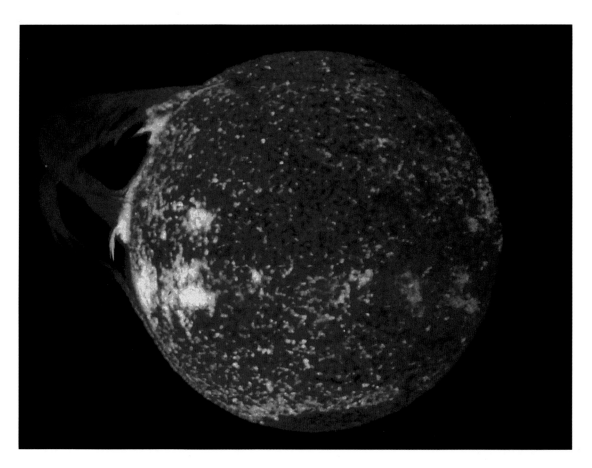

*Solar prominences jetting out from the Sun's surface are clearly visible in this photograph. This picture was taken by astronauts on NASA's Skylab space station.*

• *THE LONG JOURNEY TO EARTH* •

Sunlight is made up of tiny bits of energy called photons. In the vacuum of space, photons travel at a speed of 186,000 miles (300,000 kilometers) per second! That means that when photons leave the Sun's photosphere, they arrive at Earth in less than eight and one half minutes. But their high-speed flight through space is only part of the photon story.

Photons are created in the Sun's core as a by-product of thermonuclear fusion. Before they can shoot through space, they must first work their way out of the Sun's dense core. Scientists estimate that it can take as long as ten million years for solar photons to reach the photosphere!

---

sunspots appeared in different positions from those of the day before. The movement was very regular and always in the same direction. This meant the Sun was rotating. But scientists also noted that sunspots near the Sun's equator moved more rapidly than did those near the polar regions. This meant the Sun's surface was not solid. The Sun's middle rotates once every twenty-five days, while the regions near the Poles rotate once every twenty-five to thirty-six days.

Now imagine we are descending beneath the photosphere and toward the Sun's center. It is here that we will discover the source of the Sun's heat. As we go deeper, everything changes quickly. The temperature climbs and the pressure increases. Oddly, because the Sun's gases are so compressed, everything becomes dark.

Finally, 430,000 miles (692,000 kilometers) beneath the photosphere, we reach the center of the Sun. This is where our thermometer reaches 16,000,000°F. Our pressure gauge tells us that the pressure at the core is a billion times greater than the pressure of air at the surface of Earth. Because of that pressure, hydrogen gas in the Sun's core is compressed to 160 times the density of water. Density is just a measure of how tightly the atoms in any material are packed together. If you had two equal jars, one holding water and the other holding compressed hydrogen gas from the Sun's core, the jar of the denser compressed hydrogen gas would weigh 160 times more than the jar of water.

Under these extreme conditions, an atomic process called thermonuclear fusion is triggered. When you burn a piece of paper, chemical energy is released as heat. In thermonuclear fusion, no burning takes place. Hydrogen atoms fuse together to form helium atoms. Matter is changed and energy is released as a by-product. Every second the energy produced by this process inside the Sun is equivalent to exploding 100 billion tons (91 billion metric tons) of TNT!

It is the energy released by thermonuclear fusion that leaves the Sun to flood the solar system. This is the energy that we see on Earth as sunlight and feel as heat. This is the energy that warms Earth's oceans so that they remain liquid, drives Earth's weather, produces Earth's seasons, and powers photosynthesis, the process by which green plants produce food.

# TWO

# *THE ROCKY PLANETS*

Scientists believe that the Sun was created from a great cloud of gas, dust, and debris some five billion years ago. The gravitational attraction of all these particles pulled on one another, causing much of the matter in the cloud to fall in to the center. As matter arrived in the center of the cloud, pressure and heat climbed rapidly, and finally the Sun's nuclear furnace ignited. Our Sun became a star.

Not all the matter in the great cloud fell to the center to become part of the Sun. Knots or whirlpools of the cloud's leftovers formed at varying distances from the center. Eventually these knots gathered themselves together to become the planets. The great cloud was hottest in its center. Heavier elements in the cloud, such as iron, silicon, and oxygen, tended to condense near the center of the cloud, causing the inner planets—Mercury, Venus, Earth, and Mars—to be formed mostly from rock. Lighter elements, such as hydrogen and helium, condensed farther from the center, where it was cooler. Therefore the distant giant planets—Jupiter, Saturn, Uranus, and Neptune—are made of gas. Of the rocky inner planets, one became home to a fantastic collection of living things.

**EARTH: THE CRADLE OF LIFE**    As far as supporting life is concerned, Earth seems to be the perfect planet. It is large enough so that its gravity can hold an atmosphere. It is the right distance from the Sun so that it is neither too warm nor too cold. It has the right environment for life— liquid water and large landmasses, oxygen in its atmosphere, and a rich col-

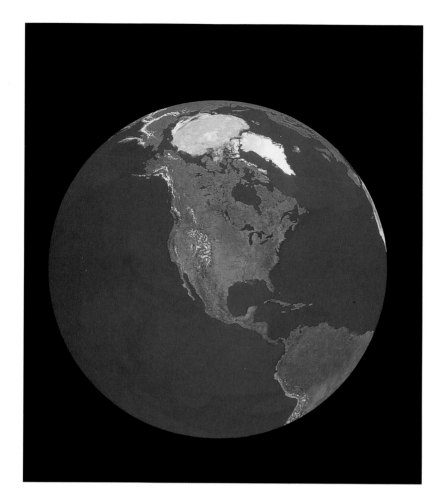

*P*lanet Earth in a view created by combining thousands of satellite photographs, each one chosen for its clarity and lack of clouds.

lection of chemicals and elements. Because of these conditions, scientists estimate that Earth is now home to millions of different kinds of plants, animals, and microbes. So far, Earth is the only planet in our solar system that is known to have life.

One of the best ways to study our home planet is from the perspective of outer space. Astronauts lift off in the Space Shuttle on the thrust of two solid propellant rocket boosters and three liquid hydrogen and oxygen propelled engines. It takes less than 15 minutes to reach a low orbit, and later, they fire the orbital-maneuvering-system rocket engines to raise the orbit to the desired level. Orbits usually range from about 130 to 360 miles (210 to 580 kilometers) above Earth's surface. They circle Earth every 90 minutes and see 16 sunrises and 16 sunsets every day. Because Earth rotates beneath

At one time or another, nearly everyone asks the question "Where did I come from?" Scientists will tell you that you came from the universe! Every atom in your body started out as matter that was created at the beginning of the universe, perhaps twenty billion years ago.

The universe began in a tremendous explosion called the Big Bang. Stars of all sizes and colors formed after this explosion and collected into galaxies.

Some of the newly created stars were short-lived and, when they began to run out of hydrogen fuel, violently exploded with the light of ten billion suns. Such explosions are called supernovas. They still occur today because new stars continue to form.

During supernovas, stars become stellar factories that manufacture elements such as carbon, silicon, iron, zinc, and gold. These elements are thrown out into space, where they collect to form new stars and planets like our Earth. Because we are creatures of Earth, we are made out of the same elements Earth is made from. That means we are all star stuff!

them, once every 24 hours, they fly over different parts of Earth's surface with every pass.

Looking out the windows, the astronauts see a wondrous sight below. On the daylight side of Earth, they see water, land, ice, and clouds. The soil and rock of the land is shaded in red, brown, yellow, black, and white. Forests and grasslands overlay the soil and rock with green and yellow. Large cities appear as bluish gray blotches that are often shrouded with a brownish pollution haze. The oceans are blue, the Arctic and Antarctic polar ice caps are white, and the tops of swirling clouds are blindingly white from reflecting sunlight. On the night side of Earth, the astronauts see brilliant light shows. The lights of countless cities flare out into space from the darkness. From above, the astronauts see hundreds of lightning strokes from widely spaced thunderstorms flashing and throbbing as the lightning jumps between clouds and land.

When the astronauts look to the horizon, they see how thin Earth's atmosphere is. The part that is visible to them is only about 50 miles (80

*The space shuttle* Columbia *lifts off into Earth orbit on July 8, 1994.*

kilometers) thick. Although the atmosphere extends out perhaps another 100 miles (160 kilometers) above the Earth, it becomes so thin that it cannot be seen or felt except by very sensitive instruments. Nearest the Earth's surface, the atmosphere appears to them deep blue, but as they look toward space, it thins out and becomes bluish gray and then black. If Earth were the size of a bowling ball, the atmosphere would be only as thick as a piece of yarn tied around it.

As thin as it is, Earth's atmosphere, along with Earth's oceans, is part of a great heat engine that helps to distribute heat from the Sun around the planet. If Earth had no atmosphere, the side of the planet facing the Sun would be over 250°F (121°C) and the side away from the Sun would be lower than -250°F (-157°C).

As far as planets go, Earth is not very big. It has a diameter of 7,926 miles (12,756 kilometers) at its equator. Earth, like all bodies in our solar system, rotates around an axis, an imaginary line running through the planet from its North to its South Pole. Earth's equator is another imaginary line that runs on the surface around Earth's middle halfway between its two Poles. Because Earth rotates, it bulges somewhat at its equator. You can see how this happens if you fill a balloon with water and then toss it up in the air with a rapid spinning motion. The balloon will bulge in the direction it is spinning. Earth's bulge is 13 miles (21 kilometers).

Earth travels in an almost circular orbit that keeps it about 93 million miles (150 million kilometers) away from the Sun. Earth's seasons are caused not by its distance from the Sun but by the tilt of its axis. Earth's axis is tilted about $23\frac{1}{2}$ degrees from its orbital path. Because of this tilt, Earth's Northern Hemisphere is angled more toward the Sun in the summer than it is in the winter. This makes the Sun climb higher in the sky and daylight last longer in the summer than in the winter, when the North Pole end of the axis is tilted away. (Seasons in the Southern Hemisphere are reversed from those in the Northern Hemisphere! When it is summer in the North, for example, it is winter in the South because the South Pole end of the axis is tilted away from the Sun.)

As the astronauts look below the Shuttle, they see that most—about 70 percent—of Earth's surface is covered by vast oceans that average about $2\frac{1}{2}$

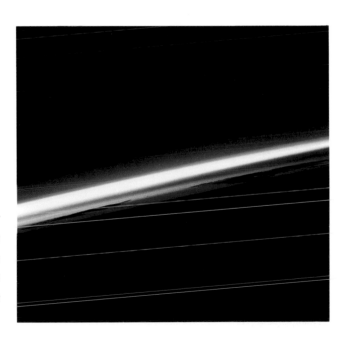

*This image of the Earth near sunrise shows the thinness of Earth's atmosphere. The black areas in the photograph are the unlit Earth (foreground) and the darkness of space (above the atmosphere).*

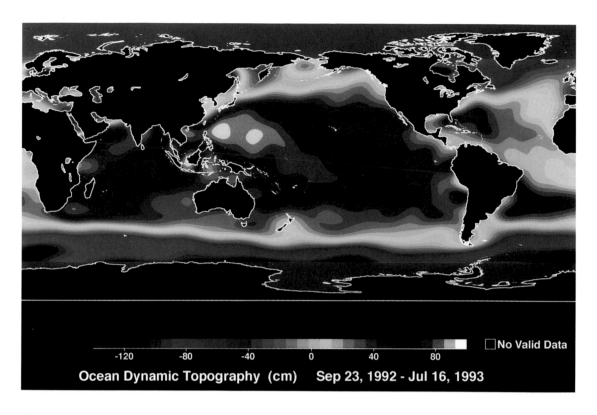

**Ocean Dynamic Topography (cm)    Sep 23, 1992 - Jul 16, 1993**

*This map shows variations in the surface of the world's oceans. Slight bulges and depressions in sea level affect ocean currents. Large-scale ocean current systems transport an enormous amount of heat around the Earth.*

miles (4 kilometers) deep. They are crisscrossed with wind-blown waves and tides driven in part by the Moon's gravitational attraction. The oceans store vast amounts of heat delivered to them by the Sun. Some of that heat causes evaporation of water into vapor. The water vapor becomes Earth's clouds, which carry moisture over the land, eventually dropping it as rain or snow.

Earth's oceans affect much of the weather experienced over the land. In winter, solar heat stored in the ocean is given up to the cooler air, causing it to rise and spread out in the upper atmosphere. As it rises, cold air from over the land moves in to take its place. This air is also warmed by the ocean, and it rises, too. A cycle of air is created. In the summer, the cycle reverses. The air above the land becomes very warm, and as it rises, cool air from over the oceans moves in to take its place. These cycles create wind, drag water vapor into the atmosphere to make clouds, and produce huge swirling weather systems that migrate around the world.

As pretty as the oceans are to the astronauts from the Space Shuttle, their eyes are drawn to the land. The land is divided into huge continents and thousands of islands scattered among the oceans. There is an odd pattern to the land that can be seen only by travelers in spacecraft at much higher altitudes, such as an *Apollo* space capsule heading toward the Moon. The continents look like a giant jigsaw puzzle. If we could shove the pieces back together, Africa would fit neatly around South America and along the eastern coast of North America. Europe and Asia would also slip neatly into the pack, and Australia and Antarctica would snuggle together near the southern ends of Africa and South America.

Scientists today know the reason for the puzzlelike appearance to Earth's continents. About 200 million years ago, the continents were joined together in one huge landmass. Because of tremendous forces, this supercontinent began to split apart into several large blocks, which moved away from one another in opposite directions. Driving this split were powerful heat-driven currents rising up from deep within the Earth.

Earth's interior has layers. The innermost is its core. It probably consists of iron and nickel and is solid in its very center, where pressure is greatest. Although it is extremely hot there, the pressure compresses the material into the solid state. About 750 miles (1,200 kilometers) from the center, the

## • PLANET OCEAN •

One of the things that strikes every astronaut who travels into space is the beauty of our planet Earth and the amount of water that covers its surface. Indeed, if you were an alien traveling into our solar system from deep space, you would have a hard time telling which planet is the one called Earth. Three-quarters of our planet's surface is covered with water. Its name should really be Ocean. Why do we call it Earth? The answer is a matter of perspective.

For thousands of years, humans thought of the land, or earth, beneath their feet as the center of the universe. They had no idea that their home was really a planet orbiting the Sun. Neither did they understand that most of it is covered with water. Since their world was covered with land as far as the eye could see, it seemed logical to them to call our home Earth. The name Earth just stuck, and it's unlikely anyone will change it now!

core is molten, or liquid. Because of movements within the liquid core, electric currents are generated, and this creates a strong magnetic field that can be measured with compasses on the Earth's surface, and in space. The molten core is about 1,400 miles (2,250 kilometers) thick.

Above the core is a wide layer called the mantle. The mantle, about 1,800 miles (2,900 kilometers) thick, extends almost to the planet's surface. Like the core, the mantle also has iron, but it has large amounts of magnesium and silicate minerals (minerals that include oxygen and silicon in their composition) as well. Because of great pressure and heat, mantle rock is solid but flows very slowly, like thick, moist clay.

Above the mantle is Earth's outermost layer—the crust. The crust varies in thickness from just a few miles under the oceans to almost 25 miles (about 40 kilometers) under the continents. The crust is made up of a wide range of different kinds of rock and minerals but is dominated by rocks containing large amounts of silicon, oxygen, and aluminum.

Earth's crust is divided into over twenty plates that are like rafts of rock floating on the denser mantle below. Large amounts of heat are generated within the mantle from radioactive decay of minerals and from friction caused by movements of matter within the mantle. Giant heat currents push upward on the crust above. About 200 million years ago some of the most powerful of these currents pushed up lava along a jagged line in the middle of the Atlantic Ocean. This caused North and South America and Europe, Asia, and Africa to be driven apart, west and east, along this line, dividing the supercontinent into pieces.

Today there is a huge mountain chain under the Atlantic Ocean that marks the jagged line and links with mountain chains under other oceans along the edges of Earth's plates. Molten lava continues to be squeezed up along the center of this line to form the mountains. Because of this, North America is moving westward at a rate about equal to the speed at which your fingernails grow.

Like a car smashing into a brick wall in a television commercial, the leading edges of the moving continents crumple to form mountain chains. The Pacific coasts of North and South America are lined with parallel mountain ranges. Similar ranges form along the opposite eastern coasts of Asia where this continent is being pushed toward the Pacific Ocean basin.

Because continental plates are of lower density, they ride over the ocean plates when the plates collide. These higher-density ocean plates are driven downward into the mantle. The friction between plates creates many earthquakes in the collision region, and many active volcanoes are found there as well.

Movements of Earth's crust, causing it to uplift, and volcanoes both create new land. But the moisture carried by the atmosphere over the continents destroys the land. Rain falling on the land forms rivers, carves and washes away rock, and deposits sediments into ocean basins. Frozen water forms glaciers that also wear away the land, but at a much slower rate. Earth's surface is the center of a dynamic "tug-of-war" between forces that build up the land and forces that tear it down. It is this tug-of-war that gives Earth the beautiful features that the astronauts see from space—mountains, valleys, plains, polar ice caps, lakes, and ocean shorelines.

Learning about the Earth is one way we learn about our solar system. With one exception, we have yet to travel in person very far from our planet. We know other worlds only by the views we get through our telescopes

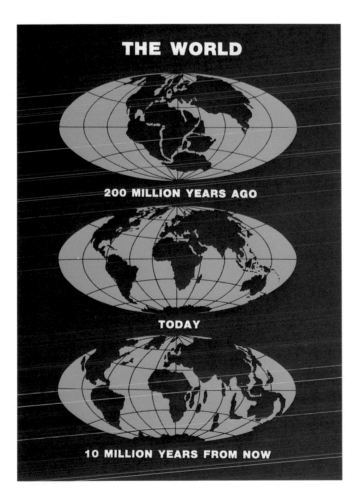

*The top map shows the supercontinent, called Pangaea, as it began to break up. The middle map shows the world as it is today. The bottom map shows changes that will occur in the future, including the drift of southern California out into the Pacific Ocean.*

and from the data sent back by space probes. Knowing what our Earth is like helps us to understand other worlds. In turn, investigating other worlds gives us new insights into our own planet.

**THE MOON: EARTH'S NATURAL SATELLITE**      After the first artificial satellites were launched in the late 1950s, the United States and the Soviet Union began manned space programs. The first humans to fly beyond Earth's atmosphere reached outer space in 1961. Several years' worth of Earth-orbital missions followed with one primary goal in mind: to place the first humans on Earth's natural satellite, the Moon. The race for the Moon was on.

The United States set about its "conquest" of the Moon by assigning the job to the National Aeronautics and Space Administration, or NASA, a new agency of the government formed in 1958. Planners at NASA knew there was much more to going to the Moon than just launching some people in a rocket toward it. They had to know some important things about the Moon before a landing could take place. For example, does the Moon have a

*This outstanding view of an entire full Moon was taken from the* Apollo 11 *spacecraft when it was about 11,500 miles (18,500 kilometers) away.*

*T*he official emblem of Apollo 11, the United States' first lunar landing mission.

solid surface, or is it covered in deep pools of dust? The answer to that question would determine how to build a lander craft.

For years, scientists have been able to study the Moon in detail through their telescopes. The Moon has light and dark areas. The light areas are full of craters, caused by impacts of space rocks or by volcanoes, and high mountains. The dark areas appeared to be smooth plains. Because the Moon is an average distance of 240,000 miles (386,000 kilometers) away from Earth, scientists couldn't be sure there were any safe landing sites on its surface.

NASA quickly prepared three different kinds of spacecraft and sent them to the Moon to get a closer look. Ranger spacecraft were like bullets that crashed into the Moon's surface. Moments before impact, they sent back television pictures which showed that the Moon had places smooth enough for landing. Although nine of these kamikaze spacecraft were launched between 1961 and 1965, only three were successful in taking pictures. From 1966 through 1968 *Surveyor* spacecraft used rocket engines to actually land on the Moon's surface. The *Surveyor*s found the surface hard enough to support a spacecraft with legs. While the *Surveyor*s were doing their jobs, Lunar Orbiters went into orbit around the Moon and used their cameras to search out possible landing sites.

The date of the first human landing on the Moon was July 20, 1969. Four days before, NASA astronauts Neil Armstrong, Edwin "Buzz" Aldrin,

HERE MEN FROM THE PLANET EARTH
FIRST SET FOOT UPON THE MOON
JULY 1969, A. D.
WE CAME IN PEACE FOR ALL MANKIND

NEIL A. ARMSTRONG
ASTRONAUT

MICHAEL COLLINS
ASTRONAUT

EDWIN E. ALDRIN, JR.
ASTRONAUT

RICHARD NIXON
PRESIDENT, UNITED STATES OF AMERICA

*The Apollo 11 astronauts left a marker behind when they completed their mission on the Moon. The plaque was fastened between the third and fourth rungs of the ladder on the lunar module's descent stage.*

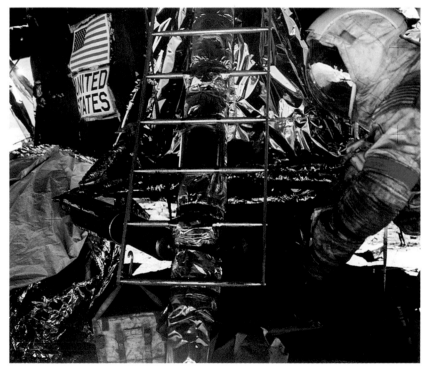

and Michael Collins blasted off for the Moon on a Saturn V rocket 363 feet (110 meters) tall. When they arrived in lunar orbit, Armstrong and Aldrin transferred into their landing craft and separated from the capsule that still contained Mike Collins. Using a powerful rocket engine to slow down the *Eagle*, their four-legged spacecraft, the two lunar explorers landed in a broad, flat area of the Moon known as the Sea of Tranquillity. While hun-

# SUMMARY OF APOLLO MISSIONS TO THE MOON

| Apollo Mission | Spacecraft CM-(Command Module) LM-(Lander) | Crew Names | Mission | Mission Dates |
|---|---|---|---|---|
| *Apollo 8* | (Not named) | Frank Borman<br>James A. Lovell, Jr.<br>William A. Anders | Orbit Moon and return | 12/21–12/27, 1968 |
| *Apollo 9* | CM—*Gumdrop*<br>LM—*Spider* | James A. McDivitt<br>Russell L. Schweikart<br>David R. Scott | Test fly lander in Earth orbit | 3/3–3/13, 1969 |
| *Apollo 10* | CM—*Charlie Brown*<br>LM—*Snoopy* | Eugene A. Cernan<br>John W. Young<br>Thomas P. Stafford | Test fly lander in lunar orbit | 5/18–5/26, 1969 |
| *Apollo 11* | CM—*Columbia*<br>LM—*Eagle* | Neil A. Armstrong*<br>Michael Collins<br>Edwin E. Aldrin, Jr.* | Explore the Sea of Tranquillity | 7/16–7/24, 1969 |
| *Apollo 12* | CM—*Yankee Clipper*<br>LM—*Intrepid* | Charles P. Conrad, Jr.*<br>Richard F. Gordon, Jr.<br>Alan L. Bean* | Explore the Ocean of Storms | 11/14–11/24, 1969 |
| *Apollo 13* | CM—*Odyssey*<br>LM—*Aquarius* | James A. Lovell, Jr.<br>John L. Swigert, Jr.<br>Fred W. Haise, Jr. | Failed to land | 4/11–4/17, 1970 |
| *Apollo 14* | CM—*Kitty Hawk*<br>LM—*Antares* | Alan B. Shepard, Jr.*<br>Stuart A. Roosa<br>Edgar D. Mitchell* | Explore the Fra Mauro Crater | 1/31–2/9, 1971 |
| *Apollo 15* | CM—*Endeavor*<br>LM—*Falcon* | David R. Scott*<br>Alfred M. Worden<br>James B. Irwin* | Explore the Hadley-Apennine mountains | 7/26–8/7, 1971 |
| *Apollo 16* | CM—*Casper*<br>LM—*Orion* | John W. Young*<br>Thomas K. Mattingly II<br>Charles M. Duke, Jr.* | Explore the Cayley-Descartes highlands | 4/16–4/27, 1972 |
| *Apollo 17* | CM—*America*<br>LM—*Challenger* | Eugene A. Cernan*<br>Ronald E. Evans<br>Harrison H. Schmitt* | Explore the Taurus-Littrow Valley | 12/7–12/19, 1972 |

*Walked on Moon

dreds of millions of people around the world watched on their television sets, Armstrong and Aldrin collected Moon rocks and soil, took many pictures, and deployed some scientific instruments to be left behind.

After several hours of rest, Armstrong and Aldrin returned to lunar orbit to dock with Collins in the *Columbia* command module. Another blast from their rocket engines sent them back to Earth for a splashdown in the Pacific Ocean on July 24, 1969.

Between 1969 and 1972 five other NASA missions carried ten more astronauts to the Moon's surface. In all, they collected 840 pounds (382 kilograms) of Moon samples. The Soviet Union never sent cosmonauts to the Moon, but it did send automatic landing craft that collected small samples of the Moon and returned them to Earth. The rock and sediment samples and all the pictures taken of the Moon have told scientists much about our nearest neighbor in space.

The Moon is a lifeless rocky world about one-quarter the diameter of the Earth. Its density is about 60 percent that of Earth. This means that the Moon's core doesn't have as much iron in it as Earth's core does. The gravitational attraction of the Moon is about one-sixth that of Earth. If you can

---

### • SAME OLD MOON •

Until satellites were sent out to orbit around the Moon, scientists knew only half the Moon's story. One side of the Moon always faces the Earth, and we couldn't see the other side. This happens because the Moon's rotation on its axis and its revolution around the Earth are exactly the same—27.3 days. Early in its history, the Moon probably rotated much faster than it does now. But gravity between the Earth and the Moon acted on the Moon, slowing its spin to what it is today.

The reason the Moon looks different every night is that the angle of sunlight falling on it is continually changing. When the Moon is between Earth and the Sun, the Moon's near side is completely in shadow. When it is on the opposite side of Earth from the Sun, its full face is completely lighted. Halfway between those two positions, we see a Moon whose near face is half lighted and half in shadow. These changing faces of the Moon's surface are called lunar phases.

*This unusual photograph, taken during the* Apollo 12 *mission, shows astronaut Charles Conrad Jr. along with two U.S. spacecraft. The* Apollo 12 *lunar module (LM) is in the background. The unmanned* Surveyor III *spacecraft is in the foreground. Here, Conrad examines the* Surveyor's *TV camera before detaching it. The camera was brought back to Earth to be examined.*

jump up 1 foot (0.3 meter) on the Earth, you could jump 6 feet (1.8 meters) on the Moon.

Having such a low gravity is one thing that prevents the Moon from having an atmosphere. An atmosphere is composed of rapidly moving gas molecules. On Earth, gas molecules cannot move fast enough to escape the planet's gravitational pull. Because of the Moon's low gravity, gas molecules can easily move fast enough to jump out into space forever. The absence of an atmosphere makes the Moon a very unpleasant place. In the sunlight, the temperature of lunar rock rises to about 266°F (130°C). In the shade, rock temperatures drop to about -274°F (-170°C). Humans can survive on the Moon only if protected by bulky space suits or sealed landing craft.

When seen from the Earth, the Moon's near side has two different kinds of surface. The lightest areas of the Moon are the highlands, consisting of

## • FLIGHTS OF FANCY •

For hundreds of years, people have told stories of fantastic voyages to the Moon. One of the earliest stories, from the second century, tells of a sailing ship and its crew that were lifted out of the water during a violent storm and blown all the way to the Moon. An eleventh-century story tells of a Persian king who lashed four lances to his throne and tied legs of lamb to the ends. Four hungry eagles were tied to the throne. As the eagles flapped their wings, trying to get to the meat, they raised the throne and the king up into the heavens. Unable to get to the meat, the eagles tired and fell back to Earth, still attached to the throne and king. A later story replaced the eagles with trained geese that were eventually successful in carrying a chair and passenger to the Moon.

Rockets were used in several stories, including one about a Chinese official named Wan Hu. Wan Hu attached forty-seven rockets to a chair fitted with winglike kites. At the fateful moment, Wan Hu's assistants lit the rockets, and there was a terrible roar. When the smoke cleared, Wan Hu and the chair were gone. Some say that he traveled all the way to the Moon.

In two of his stories, nineteenth-century French novelist Jules Verne told about a 900-foot- (275-meter-) long cannon erected in Florida that fired a bullet-shaped capsule with three passengers on board. The capsule flew around the Moon and splashed down in the Pacific Ocean. One hundred years after Verne's story, NASA astronauts traveled to the Moon from Florida on rocket power. Their capsule also carried three astronauts. When they arrived at the Moon two of the astronauts transferred from the capsule into an attached lander spacecraft. While the capsule, with one astronaut inside, continued to orbit the Moon, the lander rocketed down to the lunar surface. After the two astronauts explored the surface, the upper stage of the lander then returned to lunar orbit and docked with the command module. Leaving the lander's upper stage at the Moon, the three astronauts returned to Earth and rode their capsule to a splashdown in the Pacific Ocean. Verne's bullet capsule was named *Columbiad*. NASA's capsule was named *Columbia*!

mountains and rugged terrain. The darker areas, relatively smooth plains of old lava flows covering only about 20 percent of the total surface of the Moon, are called *maria*, a Latin word that means "seas." These are broad basins that are as much as 2 miles (3 kilometers) lower than the highlands. Although we know today that liquid water cannot exist on the Moon, the maria do resemble oceans when seen from Earth.

The most notable features of the Moon, found in both the highlands and the maria, are the thousands of craters. When satellites traveled around the Moon's far side, thousands of additional craters were seen for the first time. The far side consists almost entirely of crater-covered highlands.

The Moon's craters were created when meteoroids struck the Moon at high speed. When these space rocks hit the surface, the force and heat generated by the impact blasted out circular basins. Craters are found in all sizes from those the size of a pinhead to ones larger than the state of Connecticut. The debris from each impact created the lunar soil. Debris from some of the larger impacts splashed and formed light-colored streaks stretching outward from the craters like the spokes of a bicycle wheel.

Moon rocks come in three basic kinds. Rock found in the highlands formed when molten lava within the Moon hardened, and is light gray in color. Maria rocks consist of dark lava that flooded across the basins. The third kind of rock consists of rock and mineral fragments that were smashed by meteoroid impacts and fused together. Moon sediment consists of light or dark fragments, depending on whether it was collected in the highlands or the maria. But one kind of sediment was special. It appeared orange on the Moon when it was collected. Back on Earth, scientists discovered the sediment consisted of tiny spheres of orange glass that were created from the heat generated by meteoroid impacts.

One of the important objectives of traveling to the Moon was to try to discover how the Moon was formed. Today many scientists believe the Moon is the result of a fantastic collision of a Mars-sized planetary body with the Earth about 4.5 billion years ago. The collision threw a cloud of debris around the Earth. Gradually the debris collected into a single sphere, our Moon. As the debris collected, the Moon began to heat up and melt. Eventually the Moon cooled and formed a hard crust. Periodically volcanic eruptions welled up from cracks to flood the surface. About 4.3 billion years ago impacts of large meteoroids carved out the basins that would become

**A** *photomicrograph of a thin section of lunar sample number 70017. This Moon rock is a coarse-grained volcanic rock called basalt.*

the maria. For the next billion years, lava flowed up to the surface to fill the basins. Three billion years ago the Moon became quiet. To this day, it continues to be struck by meteoroids that grind its surface into powdery sediment and rock fragments that form a layer several yards thick.

**VENUS: PLANET OF THE CLOUDS**  In many ways, Venus and Earth are similar. Venus is a planet that is nearly the same size as the Earth. Venus has about the same density as Earth, and its surface gravity is 91 percent as strong as Earth's is. In other words, if you weigh 100 pounds (45 kilograms) on Earth, you would weigh 91 pounds (41 kilograms) on Venus. Like Earth, Venus probably has a core of iron and nickel, a mantle, and a crust. The only obvious difference between the two planets is that Venus does not have a moon. Close up, however, the differences are much greater.

Standing on Venus would not be pleasant. The surface is extremely hot, about 880°F (470°C). The planet is covered with a thick, cloudy atmosphere. Scientists using optical telescopes from Earth have never even had a single peek at Venus's surface. At the surface, the atmosphere weighs 90 times what Earth's atmosphere weighs. It is made up of about 98 percent carbon dioxide gas and has almost no water vapor. Although carbon dioxide is a gas we exhale in breathing, that much carbon dioxide is poisonous to us. To make matters worse, Venus's upper clouds are composed of sulfuric acid droplets.

Using powerful radar telescopes that can transmit radar waves to Venus, penetrate the planet's clouds, and bounce off its surface back to Earth, scientists have discovered that Venus has an unusual rotation. The planet rotates in the opposite direction from all the other planets. On Venus, the Sun rises in the west and sets in the east. Furthermore, Venus's rotation rate has been measured at 243 Earth days. This makes Venus's day longer than its year, or revolution around the Sun, since one year on Venus is 225 Earth days long. One of the consequences of its slow rotation rate is that the planet does not bulge at its equator as Earth does. Venus's equatorial diameter, 7,520 miles (12,102 kilometers), is the same as its polar diameter.

Because of Venus's nearness, it has been visited by more spacecraft from Earth than any other planet. Spacecraft have been sent to the cloud planet by the United States and the Soviet Union to fly by, orbit, penetrate its atmosphere, and land on its surface. Although each spacecraft has con-

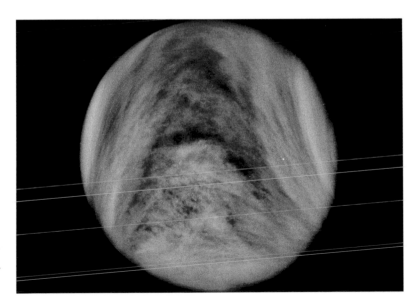

*A true-color image of the planet Venus showing the tops of clouds sweeping around the planet.*

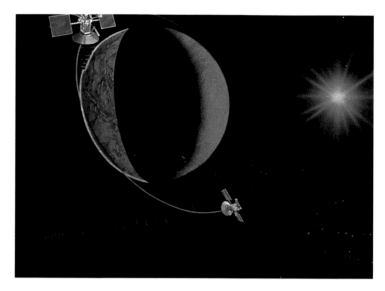

**A**n artist's rendition of the Magellan *spacecraft in orbit around Venus.* Magellan *used radar sensor equipment to penetrate the planet's dense clouds and map the surface.*

tributed to our knowledge of Venus, one spacecraft in particular enabled scientists to learn what the surface of Venus is really like.

Unlike most interplanetary spacecraft, which are launched by unmanned space vehicles, the Space Shuttle, on the 1989 STS-30 mission, was used to lift the *Magellan* spacecraft into Earth orbit. There crew members released *Magellan* so that an attached booster rocket could propel it on to Venus. *Magellan* followed a spiraling path toward Venus and fired braking rockets to reduce its speed so that it could be captured into orbit by Venus's gravity.

Because of Venus's dense clouds, there are only two ways to investigate its surface. One is to send spacecraft to land on the planet, and the other is to aim radar waves at the surface and collect their reflections to make maps. *Magellan* used radar waves, and scientists were thrilled with the results.

Venus's surface is a volcanic inferno. There are more than 400 volcanoes larger than 12 miles (19 kilometers) across. Some volcanoes look like pancakes on a griddle. Thousands of smaller volcanoes were discovered as well.

Another feature scientists were especially interested in finding were impact craters. Craters serve as a crude time clock for planetary surfaces. Scientists have estimated the rate at which planets and moons are struck by asteroids. If a planet or moon's surface is peppered with craters, they assume that the surface is very old. If the planet or moon has few craters, they conclude that something has happened to smooth the surface over. Such a surface would be considered young. *Magellan* maps of Venus showed signs of

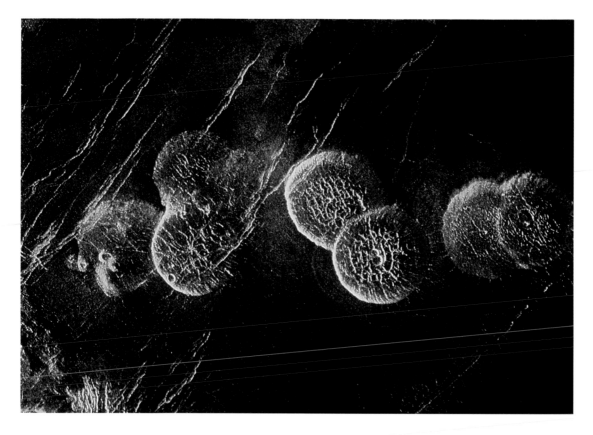

*Magellan's radar mapping shows lava domes on the surface of Venus. These flattened domes look a lot like pancakes!*

only about 900 craters, far fewer than might be expected. This indicated that the entire surface of Venus was probably covered by planet-wide lava flows about half a billion years ago.

Venus's surface is a torturous affair. It is crisscrossed by cracks and over-lapping lava flows. In places, the surface looks like hot taffy that has been twisted, pulled, folded, and compressed. The surface has strange spiderlike features consisting of circular cracks with hundreds of additional cracks stretching outward from the circle. Scientists theorize that these are places where the ground shrank after molten lava beneath the surface cooled.

Another strange feature was also detected on Venus's surface— "splotches." Venus's thick atmosphere serves as a shield to protect the sur-face from asteroids and comets falling to it from space. Only the largest of these space objects survive the heat caused by friction with the air as they enter at high speeds. Scientists believe a few larger objects nearly made it to the surface, but were ripped apart by the pressure of the atmosphere just

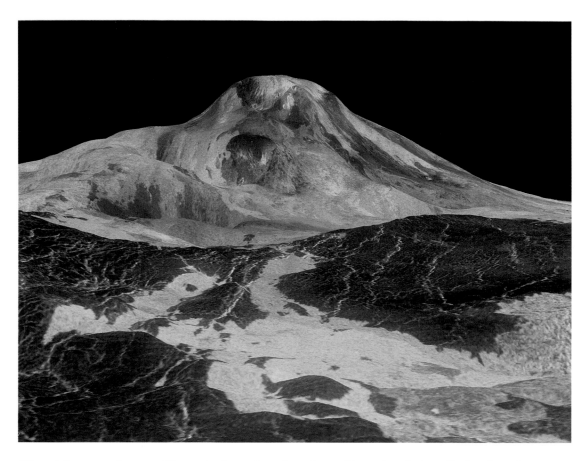

*M*aat Mons, *a volcano on Venus, is shown here in a three-dimensional view. Radar data from* Magellan *was combined with information taken from color images recorded by the Soviet* Venera 13 *and* 14 *spacecraft.*

above. Pressure waves from the objects reached the surface to jumble it up, creating a "splotch," without leaving a crater.

Studying Venus is important to learning about Earth. The planet's thick atmosphere and high temperatures combine to reduce erosion greatly there. Wind at the surface moves a sluggish 2 to 6 miles (3 to 10 kilometers) per hour, and it is much too hot for rain to fall even if there were large amounts of water in the atmosphere. Without strong winds and running water to erode the surface, ancient geological features on the planet remain fresh for study hundreds of million of years after they formed.

Another reason for studying Venus is to learn how its very hot atmosphere formed. Like the windows in a car on a hot summer day, Venus's carbon dioxide atmosphere traps the Sun's heat. A much warmer atmosphere surrounding Earth is one of the possible futures in store for us if we don't learn how to protect our environment. Learning about Venus could help us avoid that future.

## MERCURY: THE PLANETARY OVEN

Venus has had many space-craft visit it, but the Sun's innermost planet, Mercury, has had only one. That spacecraft flew past Mercury three times in 1974–1975. The space-craft, *Mariner 10*, had a two-planet mission. It first flew past Venus. While it was near Venus, that planet's strong gravitational attraction bent the space-craft's course and aimed it toward a rendezvous with Mercury. *Mariner 10*'s aim was so precise that as it whipped past Mercury, Mercury's gravity bent its path as well. The spacecraft swept into a broad orbit around the Sun. When it came back, *Mariner 10* passed by Mercury a second time and then a third time. Each time *Mariner 10* passed near Mercury, the spacecraft flew over the same terrain on the planet, giving scientists three bird's-eye views of the same part of Mercury.

Being the closest planet to the Sun, Mercury never gets very far away from the Sun's glare. The best telescope views of Mercury reveal only a dimly lit sur-face on a planet that goes through phases like the Moon. These three visits by *Mariner 10* are the only good views of Mercury scientists have ever had.

Mercury, like all other objects orbiting the Sun, travels in an elliptical path. An ellipse is a closed path that looks something like a circle that has two of its sides pushed in. You can draw an ellipse for yourself by pounding two wire nails through a sheet of paper and partly into a board underneath.

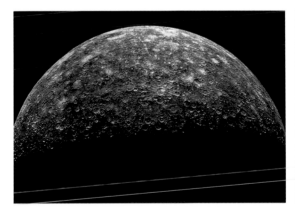 

*T*wo views of the heavily cratered surface of Mercury. The false-color image on the right was created by combining photographs taken by Mariner 10 *as it left Mercury after its first flyby on March 29, 1974.*

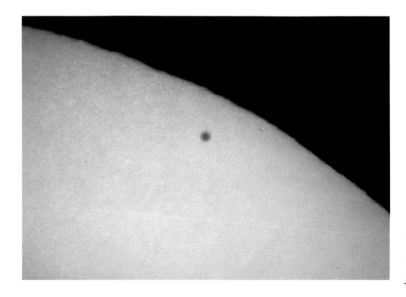

*Mercury is seen here as a small dark spot passing in front of the Sun.*

*This closeup of Mercury's surface shows that it looks very much like Earth's Moon.*

Tie a loop of string and hang it loosely around the two nails. Then push the point of a pencil inside the string loop and stretch the loop taut. If you keep the string loop tight as you trace around the loop, you will create an ellipse. If you move one of the nails closer to or farther away from the other, you will change the shape of the ellipse.

The orbits of most planets look like the ellipse you get when the two nails are very close together. Mercury's orbit looks like the ellipse you get when the nails are much farther apart. This means that Mercury's distance from the Sun varies from about 29 million miles (46 million kilometers) to 43 million miles (70 million kilometers) each orbit. Traveling around the

Sun at an average speed of 30 miles per second (48 kilometers per second), the fastest of any planet, Mercury takes 88 days to complete one orbit. Because of an odd combination of its rotation and revolution, a day on Mercury (sunrise to sunrise) takes two Mercury years to complete.

Mercury's closeness to the Sun and its slow rotation combine to give the planet another distinction. Temperatures there range more widely than on any other planet. The temperature can reach 800°F (427°C) on the Sun side, and drop to a low of -300°F (-184°C) on the dark side.

Except for Pluto, Mercury is the smallest of the planets. *Mariner 10* pictures revealed that Mercury closely resembles Earth's Moon. Like the Moon, Mercury is extensively covered with meteoroid craters and smooth plains of lava that filled big impact basins formed four billion years ago. Unlike the Moon, Mercury doesn't have distinct highland regions. Instead, Mercury has gently rolling plains that surround big impact areas. One really big impact crater on the planet is the Caloris basin, which is about 800 miles (1,300 kilometers) in diameter. The asteroid or comet that struck Mercury to make this basin sent shock waves around the entire planet. On exactly the opposite side of the planet from Caloris is a jumbled surface. The bumpiness of the surface may have been caused by the waves smashing into each other or it may be rock debris from the impact that landed there.

Studies of Mercury indicate that the planet is about as dense as Earth. This means that the planet probably has a large core of iron. At least part of the core is molten because Mercury has a weak magnetic field, the only other rocky planet besides Earth to have one.

Another feature of interest is that Mercury is wrinkled. Scientists believe that after Mercury formed, the planet became completely molten. In time, it started to cool and a hard crust formed. Asteroids and meteoroids continued crashing into the planet's surface and cracks permitted lava to flow over the surface. As Mercury's interior cooled further, the entire planet shrunk by a couple of miles. This produced wrinkles in the crust in a way similar to what happens to an apple's skin when it starts to dry.

**MARS: THE RUSTY PLANET**    After Earth and Venus, Mars has been the most studied planet in our solar system. A whole string of spacecraft has been sent to the planet to explore its intriguing surface. Certainly, a large share of interest in Mars started with an 1877 discovery of what appeared to be an intricate network of channels crisscrossing the planet's surface. Giovanni Schiaparelli, an Italian scientist, made sketches of the channels and named them *canali*, an Italian word meaning "channels." Unfortunately, newspaper reports about the discovery mistranslated the word to the English word *canal*, which implied that these features were constructed by intelligent life on Mars. For decades afterward, some scientists continued to "discover" canals and even large oases. Exciting science-fiction stories about Martians were written, and many people were convinced that Mars was inhabited by life.

From the standpoint of Mars's environment, the fourth planet out from the Sun is a good candidate for life. At an average distance from the Sun of about 1½ times farther than Earth (142 million miles, or 228 million kilo-

*T*he Valles Marineris canyon system, the largest known canyon in the solar system, is the focal point of this color-enhanced mosaic of the planet Mars.

meters), Mars's temperature ranges from just 71°F at its equator to -193°F at its south pole during winter (22 to -125°C). The Martian day is only about 37 minutes longer than Earth's, and since Mars is farther from the Sun, its year is 687 days long. Because of a tilt to its axis, Mars even has seasons as Earth does. Mars's diameter is about half that of Earth and its surface gravity is lower than Earth's. A 100-pound (45-kilogram) person on Earth would weigh 38 pounds (17 kilograms) on Mars.

The big obstacle to life on Mars is its very thin atmosphere composed mostly of carbon dioxide gas. However, even though the pressure of Mars's atmosphere at the planet's surface is about one-100th that of Earth's, it is still conceivable that life—simple plants and microbes—could exist there.

When it comes to space exploration, Mars is the hard-luck planet. Of the twenty-one spacecraft sent to Mars by the United States and the Soviet Union since 1962, thirteen failed to reach their destination, stopped working shortly after arrival, or crashed on landing. Four spacecraft, however, did a fantastic job of exploring the red planet. These were NASA's two *Viking* orbiters and two *Viking* landers that arrived at Mars in 1976. In Mars orbit, the *Viking 1* orbiter began photography of the planet's surface to find safe landing sites for the *Viking 1* lander that was attached to it.

From another very successful NASA Mars mission, *Mariner 9*, which began orbiting the planet in 1971, scientists already knew the Martian surface was fascinating. Mars doesn't have any oceans, so its surface is entirely rock. No liquid water is present anywhere on the planet because of the low

## • ONE OF OUR SPACECRAFT IS MISSING •

Seventeen years after NASA's *Viking* missions began their exploration of Mars, a powerful new Mars-bound spacecraft rocketed off Earth. The *Mars Observer* spacecraft began an eleven-month voyage in 1993, a voyage that would end when the spacecraft slipped into orbit around the red planet. There it would begin nearly 700 days of scientific study of the Martian atmosphere, planetary surface, and planetary interior.

*Launch of the* Mars Observer *spacecraft*

Three days before the spacecraft was to fire its rocket engines so that it could enter orbit, NASA controllers instructed the spacecraft to turn off its radio transmitter. This would protect the transmitter's delicate components from any shocks during pressurization of the engine's fuel tanks. Controllers waited anxiously for the transmitters to turn themselves on automatically at the end of the pressurization. Instead of a radio signal, there was silence. It appeared that something had happened to the $980 million spacecraft.

For several days, controllers tried everything they could to reestablish communications with the spacecraft, but there was no answer. Did the spacecraft explode during tank pressurization? Was it still working but had a part in its radio failed so that it couldn't respond to Earth? Had its onboard computer stopped controlling the spacecraft's function? To this day, no one knows the answer for sure. The tragedy of the *Mars Observer* was more than just a financial loss. Also lost was the chance to continue the exploration of Mars where the *Viking*s left off.

atmospheric pressure. Liquid water on Mars would immediately boil and its molecules would escape to space. However, there is frozen water beneath the soil, and large amounts of frozen water and dry ice (frozen carbon dioxide gas) at the poles as polar caps.

Mars has impact craters, volcanoes, canyons, vast plains, and small channels. Most impact craters are clustered in the Martian southern hemisphere, indicating this is the oldest surface on Mars—about four billion years old.

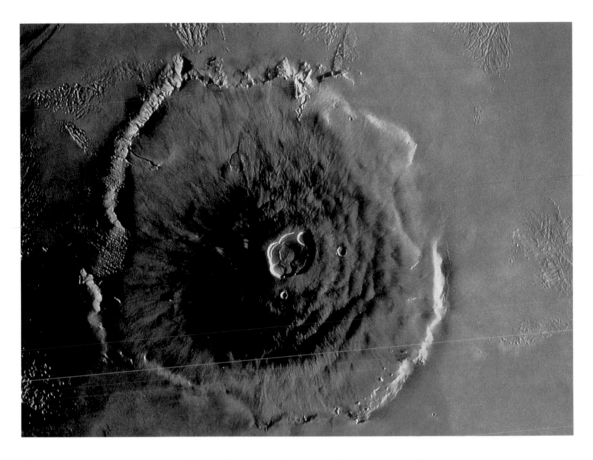

**A** *digital mosaic of Olympus Mons, the largest known volcano in our solar system*

Other areas of the planet have been covered with lava flows and have fewer craters. Just north of the equator is a 4,971-mile- (8,000-kilometer-) long ridge with several huge volcanoes running along it. All these volcanoes are larger than any found on Earth and one, Olympus Mons, is about three times taller than Mount Everest and more than 434 miles (700 kilometers) across.

The most dramatic feature on Mars is a huge canyon system, the Valles Marineris which stretches 3,000 miles (5,000 kilometers) across the surface. In places, the canyon is 430 miles (700 kilometers) across and about 4 miles (6 kilometers) deep. Earth's Grand Canyon, by comparison, would look like a small stream gully. But perhaps one of the most important discoveries about the Martian surface was the presence of hundreds of small and large channels that look as if they were cut and shaped by running water. Although none of the spacecraft could find signs of running water on the planet today, the planet could have had a thick atmosphere in the past and been very wet. The channels indicate that water once probably flowed on

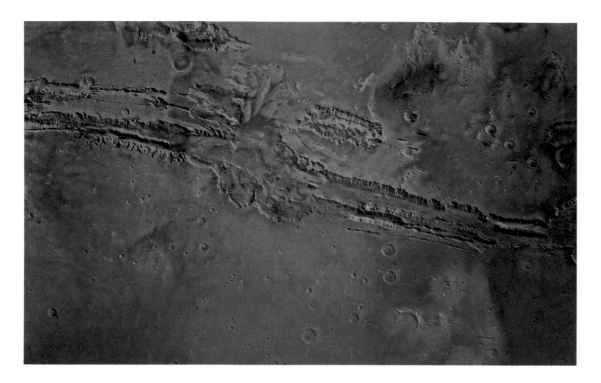

**A** *closeup of Valles Marineris*

the surface. Furthermore, bumpy chaotic terrain was discovered at the ends of the larger channels. The land was probably shaped with debris dumped on the plains during great floods. Since water is essential to life on Earth, its presence on Mars could mean that life existed there, too, and could still be present in the soil. As far as Martian canals were concerned, none were found. Scientists concluded that the canals were just scattered surface markings on Mars that looked like canals to some scientists.

While searching the surface for landing sites, the *Viking* orbiters also took time to look at Mars's two moons—Phobos and Deimos. Phobos, the larger of the two moons, is potato-shaped and is 17 miles long by 13 miles wide (27 by 21 kilometers). Deimos is about half that size. Both moons have many impact craters in their surfaces and are nearly black in color. They are thought to be rich in carbon and are probably former asteroids that were caught into Mars's orbit by the planet's gravity.

On July 20, 1976, the first *Viking* lander was ordered to attempt to land on the planet's surface. Separating from the orbiter, it used braking rockets to slow itself down and enter the thin atmosphere. An egglike shell protected the lander's delicate parts from atmospheric friction. Later a parachute

*Phobos*

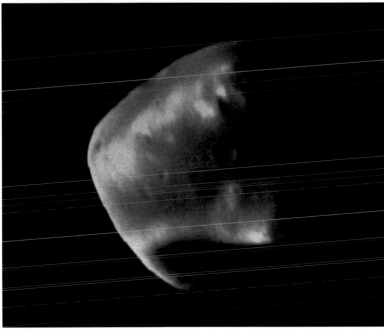

*Deimos*

popped open to slow the lander's descent. Finally the parachute separated from the craft and three clusters of small rocket engines fired for the actual landing. Spacecraft controllers waited anxiously for nineteen minutes before the radio signals from the lander finally reached Earth. Television cameras sent back their first pictures of the Martian surface. The *Viking 1* lander had settled down in a gently rolling rock-strewn and sandy plain. Colored pictures showed that the rock and soil on Mars is very orange to reddish in color, because of the presence of large amounts of iron oxide (rust).

Less than two months later, the *Viking 2* lander repeated the process

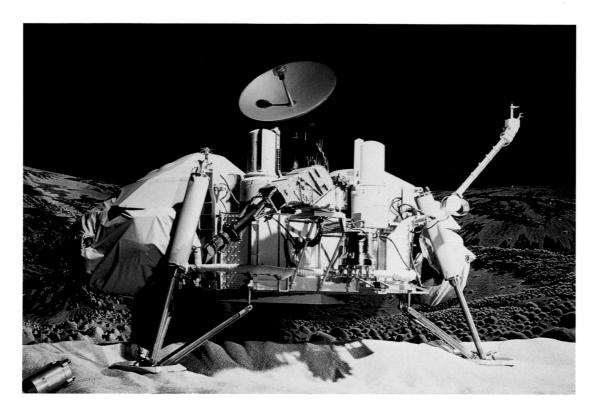

*A working model of the Mars* Viking *lander in front of a mural of what scientists thought Mars would look like. The background sky is shown as dark with a tint of blue. Mars's sky is actually pinkish.*

and landed over 4,000 miles (6,400 kilometers) to the west and north of *Viking 1*. Within days of landing, both spacecraft began searching for signs of Martian life. They each employed robot arms that scooped up Martian soil and deposited it into miniature science laboratories. Although the investigations told scientists much about the nature of the Martian surface, no signs of Martian life were detected.

Taking into consideration the environmental conditions on Mars, NASA planners believe that Mars would be a good place to send humans. First a permanent base would be established on the Moon. That could take fifteen years. Mars would be the next destination, perhaps fifteen to twenty-five years later. One of the jobs of the future explorers of Mars would be to continue looking for Martian life. The *Viking* landers could look for life only around the base of their landing footpads. Since the entire Martian surface is about equal to the total land surface on Earth, there is much land left to be explored.

# THREE

# ROCKS AND ICE BALLS

**N**ot all the gas and debris that comprised the ancient great cloud that was to become our solar system condensed into the Sun and planets. Trillions of smaller bodies formed from the remainder and never collected together to become planets. These smaller objects—asteroids, comets, and meteoroids—are scattered throughout the solar system.

**ASTEROIDS**    Asteroids are small planets ranging in size from a few yards across to an asteroid named Ceres that is over 621 miles (1,000 kilometers) in diameter. Although about 5,000 asteroids have been discovered by scientists, more than 100,000 asteroids larger than a half mile (one kilometer) in diameter are estimated to be orbiting the Sun. Asteroids may be made of various combinations of rock, metal, carbon, and water-rich clay minerals.

Most asteroids travel in an orbit, called a belt, that averages about 250 million miles (400 million kilometers) distant from the Sun. Others follow paths that cross Mars's orbit, while others even cross Earth's orbit. These asteroids are cause for some concern because they occasionally collide with planets. The Moon's maria, dark basins on the near side, are the results of asteroid collisions, and many scientists now believe the extinction of the dinosaurs on Earth may have been triggered by an asteroid impact sixty-five million years ago.

In 1991, *Galileo*, a NASA spacecraft on its way to Jupiter, passed near enough to the asteroid Gaspra to take its picture. Looking like a potato,

## • BULL'S-EYE! •

Many people speak of dinosaurs as being slow, lumbering beasts that died out millions of years ago because they were unable to adjust to Earth's constantly changing environment. Recent studies of dinosaurs indicate that they thrived on Earth for more than 160 million years before suddenly disappearing. When the dinosaurs disappeared sixty-five million years ago, so did about 70 percent of all the other life-forms on Earth. Something really big must have happened to kill off so much life on Earth!

Today many scientists believe that the "something big" was the impact on Earth of a large asteroid along the Yucatán Peninsula of Mexico. It blasted a crater that may have been up to 185 miles (300 kilometers) in diameter and threw millions of tons of rock dust and fragments into the upper atmosphere and into space. Dust blotted out the Sun's light, so that Earth was dark for many months or years. Heat waves from the blast and the steady rain of rock debris burning up on reentry into the atmosphere triggered worldwide forest fires that burned off most of Earth's vegetation. Tidal waves several miles high spread out across the Gulf of Mexico, and earthquakes were triggered around the world. In the end, no animals bigger than small dogs survived the cataclysm.

Today scientists wonder if Earth might be a bull's-eye for another asteroid or comet that is traveling through our solar system. If they could discover it with their telescopes far enough in advance, it might be possible to send rockets out to intercept it and, using atomic bombs or some other means, to deflect the asteroid or comet's course just enough so that it misses Earth.

Gaspra revealed a surface similar to those of the Martian moons Phobos and Deimos. More pictures were received when *Galileo* later photographed asteroid Ida. Both asteroids are irregular in shape and show the signs of having had numerous collisions—many craters on their surfaces.

Collisions between asteroids cause larger asteroids to become smaller and knock some fragments out of the asteroid belt. When a wayward asteroid passes near Jupiter, Jupiter's gravity bends its path and throws it out into deep space or in toward the realms of Mars and Earth. This is probably how Mars- and Earth-crossing asteroids came to be.

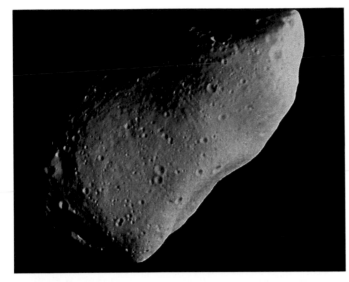

*A false-color view of Gaspra, from a photograph obtained by the* Galileo *spacecraft as it approached the asteroid on October 29, 1991.*

*This colored image gathered by the* Galileo *spacecraft shows asteroid Ida and its tiny moon (right). Taken on August 28, 1993, this picture was the first conclusive proof that an asteroid can have a satellite.*

**COMETS**   Of all the objects in our solar system, comets are among the most beautiful and surprising. Most travel in a huge elliptical orbit that brings them closer to the Sun than Earth and then farther than Uranus on the opposite limit of their orbit.

In deep space, comets are dirty ice balls consisting of frozen water, dry ice (frozen carbon dioxide), dirt, and pebbles. As they pass inside the orbit of Jupiter on their way toward the Sun, the Sun's heat warms the dry ice, causing it to release carbon dioxide gas into space. Sunlight reflects off the streaming gas. In telescopes on Earth, the comet suddenly comes into view.

### • CATACLYSM! •

Early in the day on June 30, 1908, residents in a central Siberian town called Tunguska were startled to see a brilliant blue-white fireball drop from the sky. The fireball was brighter than the Sun, and those closest to it said that the sky appeared to be covered with fire. It was so hot that it felt as if their clothes had caught fire. Then there was an explosion that could be heard more than 600 miles (1,000 kilometers) away. Trees were flattened in a circle 20 miles (32 kilometers) in diameter, the trees radiating outward from the site of the explosion. But no crater was found.

There have been many theories explaining the Tunguska fireball and explosion: an alien spaceship crashed on Earth; Earth was struck by a piece of antimatter, the stuff that helps propel *Star Trek* spaceships; or Earth was struck by a miniature black hole. Scientists believe what really happened was that Earth was struck by a comet that exploded in the upper atmosphere. It was not surprising that no nearby comets had been detected in the sky at the time, since the object approached Earth from the direction of the Sun. It would not have been visible in the Sun's glare.

There is evidence that an even greater explosion took place approximately 50,000 years ago. A massive, house-sized iron meteorite struck the desert in what is now Arizona. The force of its impact was equivalent to an explosion that would be caused if 3 million tons (2.7 million metric tons) of TNT were to go off at once. The crater left in the desert is about three-quarters of a mile (1.2 kilometers) in diameter and over 650 feet (200 meters) deep! Tourists today can easily visit the Meteor Crater, just outside the town of Winslow.

Because the Sun constantly ejects a stream of hydrogen atoms into space, these atoms act like a wind that pushes on the comet's gas to form a long and beautiful tail. Closer to the Sun, about at the distance of the asteroid belt, water ice begins to melt and water vapor starts to stream away. Dust and other debris are carried away into space with the gas. The tail becomes larger and brighter.

Some of the streaming gas from the comet forms a halo, called the

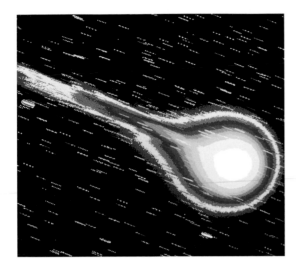

A *computer-generated, false-color image of comet Halley taken in December 1985. The nucleus of the comet is the white area at bottom right. Star trails form the background.*

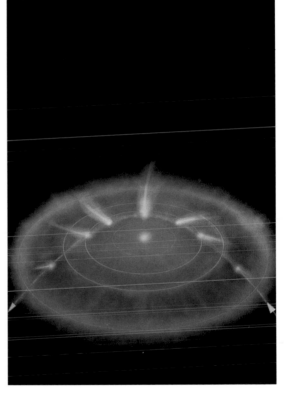

A *drawing showing the path of Halley's Comet as it rounds the Sun, crossing the orbits (orange rings) of Mars, Earth, Venus, and Mercury. The successive positions of the comet illustrate the change in length and direction of its tail as it is shaped by the solar wind. Comet Halley's orbit takes it beyond Neptune, but not as far as Pluto.*

coma, that surrounds the comet's solid part, or nucleus. In 1986 comet Halley made its most recent return to the Sun in its seventy-six-year orbit. A fleet of spacecraft from the Soviet Union, Europe, and Japan met the comet, studied its gas and debris emissions, and took pictures of its nucleus. The nucleus resembled a peanut 9 miles long by 5 miles wide (15 by 8 kilometers).

Scientists have discovered more than 900 comets passing through the solar system. They believe that comets probably formed around the Sun in the same region as Uranus and Neptune but most did not stay there.

# • COSMIC BLACK EYE •

*Scientists observing first impact*

In 1993 astronomer and comet hunter Carolyn Shoemaker noticed what appeared to be a squashed comet on a pair of pictures taken with a special camera at the Mount Palomar Observatory in California. The remarkable thing about the comet was that rather than being squashed, it was actually a train of comet pieces. Careful measurements of the movements of the pieces indicated that they had all belonged to a single comet that had passed very close to Jupiter. The planet's powerful gravitational field shattered the comet into about twenty pieces. In highly magnified pictures of the comet, the pieces formed a straight line and looked like a string of pearls. The comet was named Shoemaker-Levy 9 after Carolyn Shoemaker and amateur astronomer David Levy, who was helping Shoemaker and her husband, Gene, to search for comets.

It was determined that the comet fragments were traveling in a highly elliptical orbit and would crash into Jupiter in July 1994. Word of the impending collision spread to scientists around the world, and they planned to be ready to observe this astounding event.

Over several days, the comet fragments slammed into Jupiter just out of telescope view behind the edge of the planet. However, within minutes of the impacts, the planet rotated enough so that the effects of the high-speed collisions could be seen. Scientists were ecstatic. The aftermaths of one impact after another were clearly visible. At first the impact sites looked like dark blobs. The bigger the fragment that struck Jupiter, the bigger the blob. Later, shearing winds stretched out the blobs and made them look like curlicues. One impact made a ring-shaped mark that looked like the shiner a person gets when punched in the eye.

For a long time, scientists will study the pictures they collected of comet Shoemaker-Levy's impacts to try to learn more about how collisions affect the environments of planets. The impacts will also tell them something about what the comet fragments were made of and how dense they were.

*Multiple impacts are evident in photo taken July 22, 1994.*

**A** *meteor against a starry sky at sunset*

Because of the gravity energies of these two planets, many comets that did not stay in their domain were ejected into deep space in a region some 50 to 100,000 times the distance of the Earth to the Sun. The region is called the Oort cloud after its discoverer. Up to two trillion comets are estimated to reside in the cloud, and they take millions of years to orbit the Sun. The cloud is thought to be the source of comets that occasionally get yanked into the inner solar system by the gravity of passing stars. Without this happening, there would not be any comets for us to see. Each time a comet passes near the Sun, about a yard of its material is blown out into space. Eventually the comet melts away, leaving a small stony core that becomes an asteroid.

**METEOROIDS**    Meteoroids are bits of rock and metal ranging in size from a grain of sand to a house. They were created from the leftovers of comets and fragments formed from collisions of asteroids.

When meteoroids enter Earth's atmosphere at speeds ranging from 6 to 72 miles (60 to 116 kilometers) per second, friction with the air at an altitude of about 45 miles (70 kilometers) causes them to disintegrate into a glowing streak of light. Though they are commonly called shooting stars, their proper name is meteor. If the meteoroid is large and strong enough to survive the friction with the air, it strikes the Earth and is called a meteorite.

Every year, meteoroids add about 10,000 tons (9,090 metric tons) of matter to the Earth. Most of that matter is dust that condenses after small meteoroids burn up. Some of it comes from meteorites. Studies of meteorites indicate that about 90 percent of them are made of rock and the other 10 percent are made of iron and nickel.

# FOUR

# THE GAS PLANETS

The nature of each planet in our solar system is largely due to its distance from the Sun. As the ancient gas, dust, and debris cloud condensed and the Sun ignited its nuclear furnace, most of the lighter elements in the cloud were blown from the inner solar system by the solar wind, leaving behind mostly heavier elements that combined to form the rocky planets: Mercury, Venus, Earth, and Mars. Farther out from the Sun, lighter elements, primarily gas (hydrogen, helium, ammonia, and methane), were not nearly as affected by the solar wind and combined into the outer solar system's giant planets—Jupiter, Saturn, Uranus, and Neptune. None of these planets has a solid surface. Because of their gravitational pressures, each consists of liquid gas beneath a cloudy atmosphere. All are thought to have rocky cores in their centers.

**JUPITER: GIANT AMONG GIANTS**    Orbiting the Sun five times farther away than Earth is a planet that is larger than all the other planets, moons, asteroids, and comets combined. It is Jupiter, the center of a system of sixteen moons and a narrow banded ring of dust and debris.

Jupiter is one of the first planets the Italian scientist Galileo Galilei studied after he constructed an astronomical telescope in 1609. He discovered four of Jupiter's moons. As larger telescopes were constructed, scientists discovered more moons and reddish brown and white bands around the planet's middle. Jupiter is 88,900 miles (142,900 kilometers) in diameter and is a fast spinner. It rotates every 9 hours 50 minutes. Jupiter's fast spin causes

*Jupiter—the largest planet in our solar system*

*Voyager spacecraft, passing by Jupiter in 1979 and 1980 sent back dazzling photographs of the planet and its features.*

it to bulge at its equator. The planet's equatorial diameter is 5,761 miles (9,276 kilometers) greater than its polar diameter.

Only four NASA spacecraft have ever visited Jupiter close up. Two of those spacecraft, *Voyager 1* and *2*, carried excellent camera systems that took beautiful photographs of the planet when they passed by in 1979 and 1980. Close-up views showed that Jupiter's alternating reddish and white bands are created by winds that travel in opposite directions. The white bands, called zones, are areas where Jupiter's atmosphere is rising and condensing into whitish clouds. The darker bands, called belts, are places where the atmosphere is falling. Winds in the zones travel up to about 500 feet (150 meters) per second in the same direction as the planet is rotating. Winds in the belts travel up to about 260 feet (80 meters) per second in the opposite direction. Along the margins of belts and zones are swirling pockets of gas like the eddy currents that form in rivers on Earth. The biggest of these

*This photo montage shows the Earth floating above the clouds of Jupiter. Earth seems tiny when compared with giant Jupiter's Great Red Spot, shown in the upper right.*

**A** *false-color image of Io, one of Jupiter's moons*

swirling pockets of gas is a reddish storm called the Great Red Spot. It was first discovered in 1664 and persists to this day. Equal in size to about three planet Earths placed side by side, the Great Red Spot is a complex storm of gas swirling in a counterclockwise direction.

The *Voyager* spacecraft made many discoveries, including the fact that Jupiter has a thin ring about 18 miles (30 kilometers) wide extending around the planet almost twice Jupiter's diameter away. The ring is about 100 times fainter than Saturn's rings, which explains why it wasn't discovered until the *Voyager*s flew by.

Both *Voyager*s took many pictures of Jupiter's moon system. Pictures of Io, one of the four satellites Galileo discovered, showed that the moon had about nine volcanoes erupting at the time. Io is pale yellow in color with a hint of orange and looks like a cheese pizza. Its color comes from the high quantities of sulfur on its surface.

Europa, another of Galileo's moons, has a very smooth surface with many fine lines crisscrossing its surface. The lines look as if they have been drawn on the moon's surface with a felt marker pen. Studies of this moon indicate that it has a crust of ice about 18 miles (30 kilometers) thick that covers an ocean of liquid water that is about 30 miles (50 kilometers) deep.

*The* Voyager *mission emblem shows the spacecraft leaving Earth, traveling past Jupiter, then on to Saturn and beyond.*

The oldest-looking of Galileo's moons is Callisto. Its icy surface is very dark and relatively smooth, except for many small impact craters peppering its surface. There are also dark markings from what appears to have been asteroid impacts long ago.

Ganymede, the largest of Jupiter's moons, is a little larger than the planets Mercury and Pluto put together. Ganymede's icy surface has many craters, but it is also grooved as though someone dragged a giant rake across it. The grooves are signs that Ganymede's crust broke into great slabs that moved and pushed against one another sometime in the past.

As each of the two *Voyager* spacecraft flew by Jupiter, they caught some of Jupiter's orbital energy to change their direction and speed. Each, in turn, headed off to the planet Saturn in search of new discoveries.

## SATURN: WORLD OF MANY RINGS

Nine and a half times farther from the Sun than Earth is the second-largest planet, Saturn. Saturn is the sixth planet out from the Sun. With an intricate system of rings circling it, the planet—74,900 miles (121,000 kilometers) in diameter—looks twice as large in telescopes as it really is. Saturn takes nearly thirty years to travel around the Sun, and the tilt of its axis causes the rings to be seen edge-on at some times and fully open at others.

Aside from its beautiful appearance and some basic numbers about Saturn, we knew little about the planet until the two *Voyager* spacecraft sped by it in 1980 and 1981. Although Saturn's atmosphere, seen through telescopes, hinted at its having bands like Jupiter's, it was difficult to discern their structure. *Voyager* pictures confirmed the presence of bands but showed they are very faint. By watching clouds in the upper levels of those atmospheric bands move about, scientists calculated that wind speeds were 1,120 miles (1,800 kilometers) per hour in an easterly direction!

Scientists studying the incoming *Voyager* pictures were most interested in learning about the structure of Saturn's rings. From Earth only three rings, separated by dark gaps, were visible. Earlier NASA spacecraft, *Pioneer 10* and *11*, had flown by Saturn and added a couple more rings to the count. But *Pioneer*'s cameras were not very sophisticated, and its pictures were of poor quality. When the *Voyager*s arrived, a wonderful discovery was made.

*A true-color image of Saturn taken by the Hubble Space Telescope on December 1, 1994. A rare storm appears as a white feature near the planet's equator.*

*Hubble Space Telescope images also recorded a storm, known as the "white spot," in Saturn's atmosphere in 1990. The clouds which form the white spot are made of ammonia ice crystals.*

Instead of just a few rings with dark gaps, the photographs showed hundreds of thin rings scientists named ringlets. And the old dark gaps weren't empty at all. More ringlets were found there, but they were just too faint to be seen from Earth.

Scientists believe that Saturn's ringlets were formed from the destruction of some of the moons circling the planet. Through collisions with

### • SATURN'S EARS •

The Italian scientist Galileo Galilei was one of the first scientists to use the newly invented telescope to examine objects in the sky systematically and record observations. In 1610 he made many startling discoveries, including four moons circling Jupiter, craters and mountains on the Moon, and that Venus went through phases like our Moon does.

Because his telescope was small and its lenses were not very good in comparison to today's telescope lenses, Galileo wasn't able to see things very clearly. When he saw Saturn through his telescope, the rings looked like bumps coming out of the planet's sides. Galileo referred to the bumps as "ears."

comets and meteorites, the moons were pulverized. The resulting debris, from grains the size of dust to house-sized icy particles, spread out around the planet. Saturn's gravity and that of the remaining satellites shaped the particles into ringlets.

The structure of the ringlets was amazing to the scientists who studied the *Voyager* pictures. They spotted kinks in some of the ringlets and concluded that the gravitational pull of two of Saturn's small moons was tugging on the ringlet particles, causing the kinks. Some rings were spiral-shaped, like phonograph record grooves. Spokelike structures were also discovered. These were dark shadows that appeared over the ringlets and pointed out into space. Scientists theorized that the spokes were some-

**A** *highly enhanced color view of Saturn's rings. Color variations may be the result of differences in the chemical composition from one part of Saturn's ring system to another.*

how the result of static electricity and that Saturn's magnetic field caused dust particles to float over the rings in dark, shadowy lines.

Also of great interest were *Voyager* encounters with Saturn's moons. *Voyager* increased Saturn's moon count from ten to eighteen.

Titan, a planet-sized moon that is larger than Mercury or Pluto, was fascinating to scientists. This moon has its own atmosphere, which is about $1\frac{1}{2}$ times thicker than Earth's. The atmosphere is very cold, -290°F (-179°C) and is made up of nitrogen and methane. Scientists think that sunlight causes some of the atmosphere to convert chemically to compounds similar to ethane that fall to the hard surface like rain or snow and accumulate in lakes. Recent pictures taken of Titan by NASA's Hubble Space Telescope have revealed what could be a continent on Titan the size of Australia. Surrounding it may be a sea of tar.

Saturn's satellite Enceladus has huge cracks and valleys. At some time in its past, Enceladus's crust probably shifted about as Earth's crust still does. The floors of the cracks and valleys may be filled with frozen water that spilled out onto the moon's surface from its interior. Mimas, another moon, is lucky to be around. It was struck by a comet or small moon with such force that it nearly split in two. Tethys, still another satellite, has a valley 1,240 miles (2,000 kilometers) long that stretches three-quarters of the way around its surface.

Completing their work at Saturn, the two *Voyager*s left on separate paths. *Voyager 1*'s planetary encounters were over, and it began a new mis-

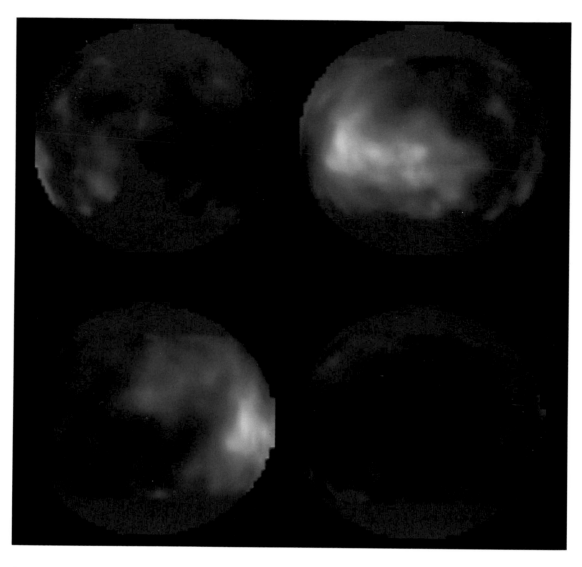

*Four views of Titan, one of Saturn's moons. The image in the upper right shows a bright surface feature about as large as the continent of Australia.*

sion to travel out of the solar system into deep space. It is measuring the Sun's solar wind to see how far into space it extends. *Voyager 2*'s path headed in a different direction. Using Saturn's motion and gravitational pull, *Voyager 2*'s path was redirected toward an encounter with the seventh planet, Uranus.

**URANUS: THE BULL'S-EYE PLANET**   Nine years before *Voyager 2*'s 1986 arrival at Uranus, scientists flying in a high-altitude jet plane with a telescope mounted on board discovered a very faint ring system circling the planet. The scientists didn't actually see the rings themselves. Instead, they saw shadows the rings cast as Uranus passed in front of a distant star. Later, when *Voyager 2* reached Uranus, it measured the brightness of the rings. Only about 2 percent of the sunlight that falls on them reflects back, explaining why they couldn't be seen directly through a telescope. *Voyager* pictures of the rings indicated that they are made of boulder-sized particles of some very dark material. The rings are thin, less than 30 miles (48 kilometers) wide on the average. In pictures, the rings look like white pencil lines drawn on black paper.

If we could see Uranus's rings through a telescope, the planet would look like a bull's-eye at certain times during its orbit around the Sun. This happens because of the unique tilt of Uranus's axis. Unlike the other planets, which have their spin axes aimed more or less perpendicular to their orbits, Uranus's axis is parallel to its orbit. It's as though Uranus is lying on its side. Because of this, Uranus's north pole points almost directly at the

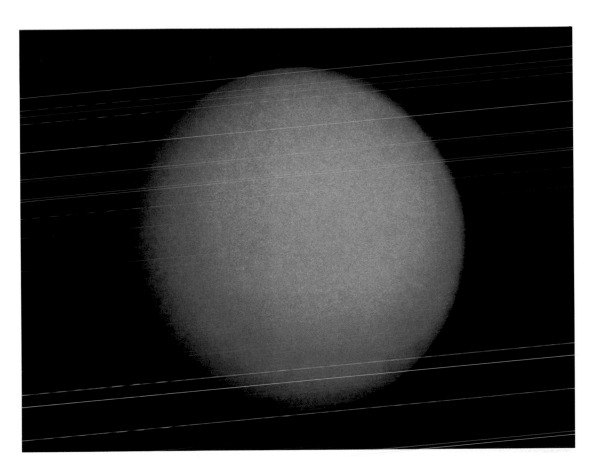

**A** *color composite of the planet Uranus returned by the camera of* Voyager 2

Sun once every Uranus year. (A Uranus year is eighty-four Earth years long.) One-half of a Uranus year later, with the planet on the opposite side of the Sun, the south pole points in the Sun's direction. Because Uranus's rings circle the planet's equator, Uranus looks like a bull's-eye when either pole points toward the Sun.

Uranus is four times bigger than Earth, which makes it the third largest planet. It has a dense atmosphere that gives the planet a blue-green color visible even through small telescopes on Earth. Some of the chemicals in the atmosphere appear to undergo a reaction, triggered by sunlight, to produce a haze that may be similar to the pollution smog that covers cities like Los Angeles during some seasons of the year.

*Voyager 2* didn't detect any strong bands in the atmosphere of Uranus, but it did measure very strong wind speeds. Near Uranus's equator, the winds zip along at speeds of up to 650 miles (1,042 kilometers) per hour.

Although *Voyager 2*'s cameras couldn't see very far into the cloudy atmosphere of Uranus, scientists estimate that the atmosphere is about 5,000 miles (8,000 kilometers) thick. Beneath the atmosphere is probably an ocean of water and ammonia, and beneath that is an Earth-sized core of heavier materials.

Before *Voyager 2* arrived at Uranus, scientists knew of only five moons circling the planet. By the time the spacecraft left for its next destination, ten more moons had been added to the list. All of the new moons are small, less than 90 miles (145 kilometers) in diameter, and are very dark in color. They are as black as a lump of coal on a snowbank.

Uranus's large moons range in size from Miranda, 293 miles (472 kilometers) in diameter to Titania, 981 miles (1,580 kilometers) in diameter. Miranda is a strange world marked with craters, large cracks, and two large oval features that look like racetracks. Ariel has long cracks in its surface and flat areas that appear to have been filled in with lavalike flows of water ice mixed with ammonia and methane. Umbriel looks as if the surface is covered with a thin coating of some dark material. Umbriel also has a strange, whitish doughnut-shaped oval with a mountain peak in its center. Titania's icy surface, although heavily cratered, has few large craters. In the solar system's early history, large crater-forming impacts were very common. Scientists speculate that Titania probably was hot enough to melt and smooth out the large impacts. As a result, only the more recent small impact craters are still present. Titania also has large cracks that extend hundreds of

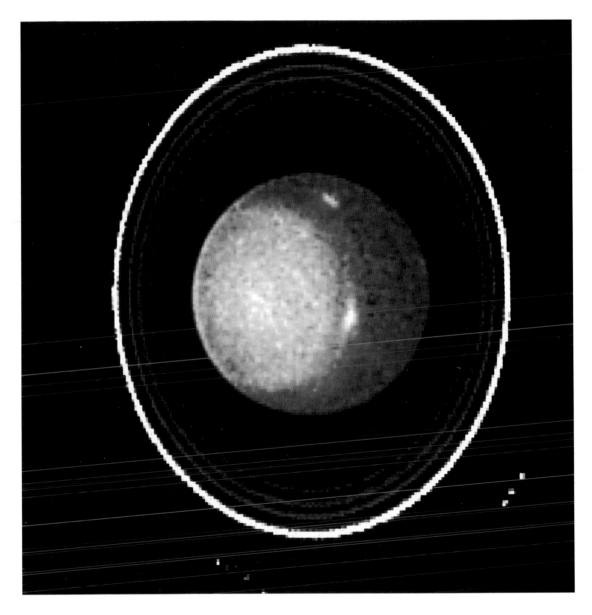

**A** *composite Hubble Space Telescope image of Uranus appearing as a bull's-eye within its rings.*

miles. Oberon, the farthest away of Uranus's moons, is similar in appearance to Titania. It is heavily cratered and has an icy surface.

Once again, *Voyager 2* took advantage of a planet's motion and gravity to change its course for another encounter. This time, it was off to Neptune!

### NEPTUNE: LAST OF THE GAS GIANTS
For about twenty out of Neptune's 165-Earth-year-long orbit, it is the farthest planet from the Sun.

This happens because Pluto's orbit is the most elliptical of all the planets in the solar system. When it is approaching the nearest point to the Sun in its orbit, Pluto actually gets closer to the Sun than does Neptune. When *Voyager 2* passed by Neptune in 1989, Neptune was the farthest planet from the Sun.

Circling the Sun at a distance thirty times farther away than Earth, Neptune receives only about one-900th the sunlight Earth does. With little energy being delivered to Neptune from the Sun, scientists expected the planet to be a rather quiet and boring world compared with Jupiter. The reverse was true. Neptune turned out to be a dynamic world. *Voyager 2* pictures of Neptune revealed a bluish atmosphere with faint bands. By comparing the movements of clouds between successive *Voyager* pictures, scientists determined that winds in the upper atmosphere were traveling westward at speeds of up to 1,240 miles (2,000 kilometers) per hour.

Like Jupiter, Neptune had swirling storms moving about it. One storm, named the Great Dark Spot, was a huge storm similar to Jupiter's Great Red Spot. Rather than being red in color, it was darker blue than the rest of Neptune's atmosphere and about the size of the Earth. There was also an irregularly shaped white cloud that scooted around the planet every sixteen hours or so. Scientists named the cloud Scooter. Other white clouds high in Neptune's atmosphere are similar to the high wispy cirrus clouds often seen on Earth.

Neptune, like the three other giant planets, also has rings. Five faint rings similar to those that surround Uranus circle Neptune. They are also made of dark particles but have their own unique characteristics as well. In several places there is a greater collection of particles than in others. This makes the rings look fatter and brighter in those places. Scientists called these places ring arcs.

Thanks to *Voyager 2*, Neptune is now known to have eight moons. Only two moons were known before the spacecraft's visit. The new moons are all small and dark. Triton, Neptune's largest moon, is about three-quarters the size of Earth's Moon. It turned out to be one of the most remarkable objects *Voyager 2* visited during its entire journey.

Triton orbits Neptune in an unusual way. It travels in a backward direction from the other seven Neptunian moons. Its orbit is also tilted by about 20 degrees compared to the orbits of the other moons. This suggested to

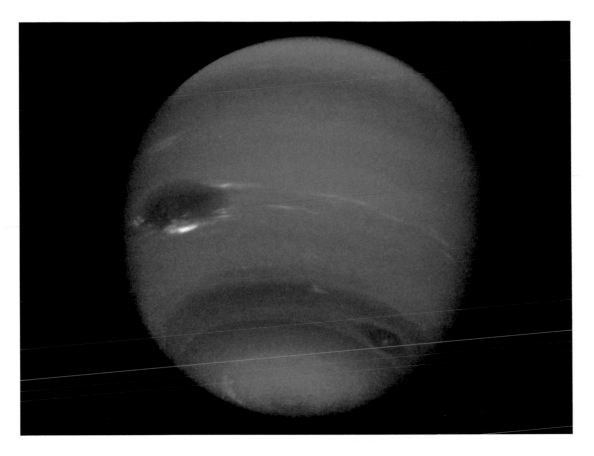

*Images returned by* Voyager 2 *have revealed much new information about Neptune.*

scientists that Triton was not one of Neptune's original moons. Instead, it may have formed somewhere else in the solar system and been captured by Neptune's gravity.

Triton's surface temperature, -391°F (-235°C), is the lowest of any planet or moon in the solar system. Its icy surface is relatively smooth and has an odd pattern that resembles the texture of the outside of a cantaloupe. *Voyager 2* recorded some thin dark plumes rising upward like smoke from the moon's surface. Scientists knew Triton had a very thin atmosphere, and *Voyager 2* permitted them to see its effects. These plumes were from geysers erupting on Triton. The geysers were blasting nitrogen gas and dark dust particles high into Triton's atmosphere. High-altitude winds sheared off the plumes and blew them over the moon's surface.

Neptune was *Voyager 2*'s last major objective. As it flew past the planet, it traveled out into deep space to join *Voyager 1*'s search for the edge of the

Sun's domain. Although one planet was left to explore, Pluto was just not in the right position for *Voyager 2* to reach it. Yet *Voyager 2* did provide scientists with an idea of what Pluto might be like. It is likely that Pluto and Triton are very similar bodies and exploring one might tell us something about the other.

# FIVE

# PLUTO AND WORLDS BEYOND

For most of its 248-year-orbit around the Sun, Pluto is the most distant of the Sun's planets. On the average, its orbit is 40 times farther from the Sun than Earth's. But because its orbit is very elliptical, Pluto can approach as close as 30 times Earth's distance from the Sun. At other times, Pluto may be as far away as 50 times Earth's distance from the Sun.

Pluto has a diameter of just 1,416 miles (2,280 kilometers), making it the smallest of the planets. In fact, six of the moons in the solar system are actually bigger than Pluto.

Considering its small size and great distance from the Sun, it is not surprising that Pluto was the last planet discovered. It was discovered by an Illinois farm boy who would later become a scientist at the Lowell Observatory in Flagstaff, Arizona. Twenty-one-year-old Clyde Tombaugh was assigned the job of methodically searching the skies for a new planet. The observatory's founder, Percival Lowell, had predicted that the new planet existed and even predicted the general area in the sky where it might be found. In 1930 Tombaugh discovered a tiny dot on a star picture he had taken. Comparing this picture to another taken of the same place in the sky six days earlier, Tombaugh discovered the dot had moved. It was Lowell's planet—the first new planet discovery in eighty-four years.

Until recently, little was known about Pluto. It was just too small in telescopes to make out much detail. But in 1978 a fuzzy picture taken of Pluto revealed that the planet has a companion moon that is half Pluto's diameter. The moon's size was unusually large for such a small planet. It was

*Pluto is at the center of the frame while Charon is the fainter object in the lower left of this Hubble Space Telescope image. The fuzzy picture was taken before the telescope's optical problem was fixed.*

named Charon. Because of the similarity in the sizes of Pluto and Charon, scientists began to think of the two as a double planet.

Ten years later, another important discovery was made about Pluto. From the way a distant star's light flickered as Pluto passed in front of it, scientists determined that Pluto has an atmosphere. The atmosphere is very thin and is probably composed of nitrogen, carbon monoxide, and methane gas. The atmosphere is probably temporary. When the discovery was made, Pluto was near its close point to the Sun. The gas seemed to come from Pluto's surface ice as the Sun warmed it. Farther from the Sun, where it is colder, the gas release will probably stop. The thin atmosphere will refreeze and fall back on the surface until the next time Pluto comes near the Sun.

So far, no spacecraft has ever come near Pluto. NASA is planning a mission to the planet, but, for the time being, scientists have to be satisfied with telescope pictures of it. One especially good picture was taken by NASA's Hubble Space Telescope. The picture showed Pluto and Charon separated from each other. That was something the best Earth-based telescopes could not do.

We still know little about Pluto and Charon. Pluto's surface may be similar to the surface of Neptune's moon Triton. It is covered with methane ice, while Charon is probably covered with water ice. Both bodies are believed to have rocky cores.

**THE LAST PLANET?**     It is hard to say if Pluto is the final planet in our solar system. Scientists have wondered if there are others. One suggestion is that there may be a planet orbiting the Sun closer than Mercury. The yet-to-be-discovered planet has even been named—Vulcan. Another idea is that there may be a planet traveling the same orbit around the Sun as the Earth. By chance, this planet is exactly on the opposite side of the Sun from Earth. We never get to see it because as we orbit around to the far side, the mystery planet orbits around to our side. As of yet, there is no evidence pointing to either planet's existence.

Scientists have also wondered if there are planets farther from the Sun than Pluto. Scientifically, deep-space planets seem more likely. The two *Voyager* spacecraft and two earlier spacecraft, *Pioneer 10* and *11*, have now moved far enough out into space that a new planet's gravity could affect their course if they came near it. If the spacecraft's paths are bent, there would be strong evidence that there is at least one more planet out there. So far, none of the spacecraft have deviated from their courses. This doesn't mean that

---

### • ASTRONOMER ASTRONAUT •

Scientists come in all forms. One kind of scientist is the astronomer, who studies stars, galaxies, and other objects out in space. Some astronomers like nothing better than spending long nights in lonely mountaintop observatories directing telescopes. Others spend much of their time at computer terminals analyzing data from telescopes and spacecraft. One astronomer, Jeffrey A. Hoffman, has decided to visit outer space himself.

Jeff Hoffman is a NASA Space Shuttle astronaut. His astronomy specialty is high-energy cosmic gamma ray and X-ray studies. As an astronaut, he has flown four times in space. On the 1990 STS-35 mission, Hoffman was a part of the crew that operated the ASTRO-1 ultraviolet astronomy instruments carried in the Shuttle's payload bay. His most recent mission had him space-walking three times as he worked outside the Space Shuttle to help repair the Hubble Space Telescope. Jeff Hoffman knows what it is like to see the stars without Earth's atmosphere getting in the way.

Pluto is the last planet in our solar system. On the contrary, there may be hundreds of mini-planets orbiting the Sun well beyond Pluto. Some of these bodies have already been detected by astronomers using very sensitive telescopes. The mini-planets appear to be chunks of ice and dirt less than a few hundred miles in diameter.

What about planets outside of our solar system? Are there other solar systems? So far, no other solar systems around distant stars have actually been seen by even our most powerful telescopes. However, small jiggles in the movements of some stars indicate they have unseen bodies orbiting them. These bodies could be Jupiter-sized planets. Recent studies of a distant rapidly spinning star indicate that it has three planets circling it.

For the time being, until we can actually take pictures of other solar systems, we have to be satisfied with making estimates about them. Just looking at our own Milky Way galaxy, we find that it is home to at least 100 billion stars. If just one in a million stars had planets of its own, that would mean

*The Milky Way shows clearly in the night sky over Pike's Peak, Colorado.*

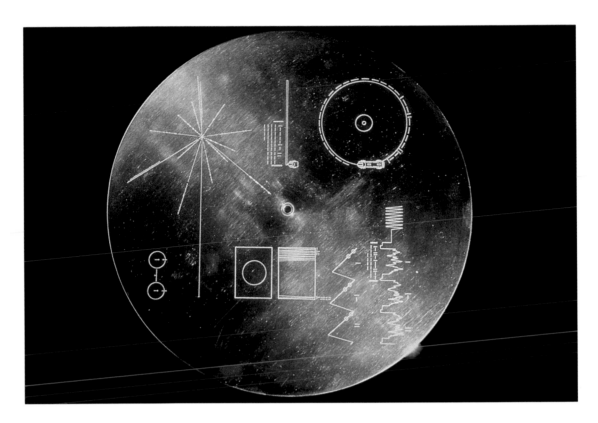

*Each of the two* Voyager *probes carry a record called the "Sounds of Earth." The messages on the record were designed to help possible extraterrestrial civilizations, who might intercept the spacecraft millions of years from now, to put together some picture of twentieth-century Earth and its inhabitants.*

that there are at least 100,000 solar systems in the Milky Way. However, some scientists estimate the number to be much higher—about half of the stars, or 50 billion, have solar systems of their own!

All this leads us to a tough question. Are we alone? The basic chemical elements required for life are found throughout the universe. But there are so many factors that make a planet suitable for life that life, especially intelligent life, may be rare. Until we are visited by aliens in a "flying saucer," something that hasn't happened yet regardless of what supermarket tabloids say, we have to try to answer the question with radio telescopes.

The radio and television programs we broadcast around Earth also spill out into space. If there were intelligent creatures on other worlds wondering if *we* exist, they would use radio telescopes to search for our signals.

For several years, Earth scientists have done just the same to search for alien radio transmissions. So far, no artificially produced extraterrestrial radio signals have been detected. We may never find such signals, but the important thing is that we keep trying.

The launch of *Sputnik 1* in 1957 was the beginning of the age of space exploration. It has led to wonderful discoveries. Even so, we have still only just begun to understand Earth's place in the solar system and the universe. And, with perhaps 50 billion solar systems in the Milky Way galaxy left to explore, it is an adventure that will never end.

# A BRIEF GUIDE TO PHOTOS FROM SPACE

For more than thirty-five years, robot spacecraft and astronauts have been gathering data about our solar system through photography and electronic imaging systems. Once back on Earth, these pictures are studied intensely to gain the information they contain. Much of the information presented in this book is based on such pictures.

As you read the picture captions, you encountered a variety of terms such as *false color*, *digital mosaic*, and *photomicrograph*. What do these terms mean? The list below will give some definitions. However, before reading it, it is important to understand the two main ways pictures are brought back to Earth. In the early days of space exploration, most pictures were photographs collected on film by astronauts as they orbited Earth. The exposed film was simply brought back to Earth for developing and examination. However, as spacecraft were launched to the Moon and the planets, it became obvious that using film was impractical. These spacecraft were sent out on one-way trips so that it would not be possible to return the film. Instead, electronic systems, (similar to television pictures) were used to collect images and then radio them back to Earth. Because these images are electronic, computers are able to process the images in a variety of ways to gain as much information from them as possible.

**Composite**—Several images taken of the same object but with different filters are combined together. For example, if three images are taken of Jupiter with red, green, and blue filters, the individual images each reveal something different about the planet. However, when the images are combined together to make a composite, a true-color image is produced.

**Computer enhanced**—Electronic images that have been changed by computers to bring out details that are not easy to see. This is similar to adjusting the color and brightness controls on a television set.

**Digital mosaic**—A mosaic created on a computer screen in which several images are combined together. Because the images are digital (computer numbers), the separate images can be blended so no seams are visible.

**False color**—An electronic image whose color has been changed to bring out subtle detail. For example, a scientist might want to study small bodies of water in an Earth picture. The scientist will program the computer to show water as bright red so it is easy to pick out from the picture.

**Image**—A picture created of an object by collecting light from it and converting the brightness of that light to computer numbers that are later processed into the image.

**Mosaic**—Two or more images or photographs of a large object that have been pasted together to form a larger image. This is necessary when a single camera view cannot cover the entire object.

**Photograph**—A picture created of an object by exposing film to light and developing it with chemicals.

**Photomicrograph**—A picture of an object taken through a microscope.

**Photo montage**—A picture in which several objects are brought together for comparison. For example, the picture of Earth and Jupiter's Great Red Spot on page 65 is a photo montage.

**Photo mosaic**—Mosaic created by pasting photographs together.

**Three-dimensional**—A flat (two-dimensional) picture that is processed to look like it has depth (three dimensions). Often, these images are exaggerated to make details easier to see, such as making mountains look taller than they actually are.

**True color**—A photograph or image that appears as the human eye would see it.

**X ray**—One of the many forms of light found in the electromagnetic spectrum. X rays are an invisible form of light that can be made visible by exposing X-ray sensitive film to X rays. X rays can tell astronomers about extremely powerful events, such as giant explosions on the Sun.

# PLANETARY DATA

| Planet | Distance from Sun in A.U.[1] | Orbital Period (Earth years) | Rotation (Earth hours)[2] | Equatorial Diameter (Miles and kilometers) | Mass (Earth = 1)[3] | Density (Water =1)[4] |
|---|---|---|---|---|---|---|
| Mercury | 0.387 | 0.24 | 1,408 | 3,030 4,878 | 0.06 | 5.4 |
| Venus | 0.723 | 0.62 | 5,832R | 7,520 12,102 | 0.82 | 5.3 |
| Earth | 1.0 | 1.0 | 23.93 | 7,926 12,756 | 1.0 | 5.5 |
| Mars | 1.524 | 1.88 | 24.62 | 4,220 6,794 | 0.11 | 3.9 |
| Jupiter | 5.203 | 11.96 | 9.92 | 88,849 142,984 | 317.89 | 1.3 |
| Saturn | 9.555 | 29.46 | 10.66 | 74,900 120,536 | 95.18 | 0.7 |
| Uranus | 19.218 | 84.01 | 17.24 | 31,022 49,946 | 14.54 | 1.2(?)[4] |
| Neptune | 30.108 | 164.8 | 16.11 | 30,236 48,680 | 17.15 | 1.7(?)[4] |
| Pluto | 39.439 | 247.7 | 153.3 | 1,416 2,280 | 0.002 | 0.3-0.8(?)[4] |

[1] The distance from the Earth to the Sun is called an astronomical unit, or A.U. To find out the distance to any planet in miles, multiply the A.U by 93 million. To find out the distance in kilometers, multiply by 149 million.

[2] R indicates that the planet rotates in a direction opposite to all other planets.

## PLANETARY DATA

| Planet | Surface Gravity (Earth = 1) | Surface | Atmosphere | Number of Moons | Number of Rings |
|---|---|---|---|---|---|
| Mercury | 0.38 | Rock | None | 0 | 0 |
| Venus | 0.91 | Rock | Carbon Dioxide, Sulfuric Acid | 0 | 0 |
| Earth | 1.0 | Rock, Water, Ice | Nitrogen, Oxygen, Water | 1 | 0 |
| Mars | 0.38 | Rock, Carbon Dioxide Ice, Water Ice | Carbon Dioxide | 2 | 0 |
| Jupiter | 2.54 | None | Hydrogen, Helium, Methane, Ammonia | 16 | 1 |
| Saturn | 1.07 | None | Hydrogen, Helium, Methane, Ammonia | 18 | Thousands |
| Uranus | 0.88 | None | Hydrogen, Helium, Methane | 15 | 11 |
| Neptune | 1.14 | None | Hydrogen, Helium, Methane | 8 | 5 |
| Pluto | 0.05 | Nitrogen Ice, Water Ice, Carbon Dioxide Ice | Nitrogen | 1 | (?)[4] |

[3] Earth's mass in pounds is the number 13,175 followed by 21 zeros. Earth's mass in kilograms is the number 5,976 followed by 21 zeros.

[4] Question marks indicate a value is not known for certain.

## SUCCESSFUL INTERPLANETARY SPACECRAFT

| Spacecraft | Nation | Launch | Arrival | Target | Notes |
|---|---|---|---|---|---|
| *Mariner 2* | USA | 1962 | 1962 | Venus | Flyby* |
| *Mariner 4* | USA | 1964 | 1965 | Mars | Flyby |
| *Venera 4* | USSR | 1967 | 1967 | Venus | Lander |
| *Mariner 5* | USA | 1967 | 1967 | Venus | Flyby |
| *Venera 5* | USSR | 1969 | 1969 | Venus | Lander |
| *Venera 6* | USSR | 1969 | 1969 | Venus | Lander |
| *Mariner 6* | USA | 1969 | 1969 | Mars | Flyby |
| *Mariner 7* | USA | 1969 | 1969 | Mars | Flyby |
| *Venera 7* | USSR | 1970 | 1970 | Venus | Lander |
| *Mariner 9* | USA | 1971 | 1971 | Mars | Orbiter |
| *Mars 2* | USSR | 1971 | 1971 | Mars | Orbiter, lander crashed |
| *Mars 3* | USSR | 1971 | 1971 | Mars | Orbiter, lander crashed |
| *Pioneer 10* | USA | 1972 | 1973 | Jupiter | Flyby |
| *Venera 8* | USSR | 1972 | 1972 | Venus | Lander |
| *Pioneer 11* | USA | 1973 | 1974 | Jupiter | Flyby |
| Continued on to | | | 1979 | Saturn | Flyby |
| *Mars 5* | USSR | 1973 | 1974 | Mars | Orbiter |
| *Venera 9* | USSR | 1975 | 1975 | Venus | Lander |
| *Venera 10* | USSR | 1975 | 1975 | Venus | Lander |
| *Viking 1* | USA | 1975 | 1976 | Mars | Orbiter and lander |
| *Viking 2* | USA | 1975 | 1976 | Mars | Orbiter and lander |
| *Voyager 1* | USA | 1977 | 1979 | Jupiter | Flyby |
| Continued on to | | | 1980 | Saturn | Flyby |

* First successful interplanetary mission
USA: United States of America
USSR: Soviet Union

## SUCCESSFUL INTERPLANETARY SPACECRAFT

| Spacecraft | Nation | Launch | Arrival | Target | Notes |
|---|---|---|---|---|---|
| *Voyager 2* | USA | 1977 | 1979 | Jupiter | Flyby |
| Continued on to | | | 1981 | Saturn | Flyby |
| Continued on to | | | 1986 | Uranus | Flyby |
| Continued on to | | | 1989 | Neptune | Flyby |
| *Pioneer 12* | USA | 1978 | 1978 | Venus | Orbiter |
| *Pioneer 13* | USA | 1978 | 1978 | Venus | Five landers |
| *Venera 11* | USSR | 1978 | 1978 | Venus | Flyby and lander |
| *Venera 12* | USSR | 1978 | 1978 | Venus | Flyby and lander |
| *Venera 13* | USSR | 1981 | 1982 | Venus | Flyby and lander |
| *Venera 14* | USSR | 1981 | 1982 | Venus | Flyby and lander |
| *Venera 15* | USSR | 1983 | 1983 | Venus | Orbiter |
| *Venera 16* | USSR | 1983 | 1983 | Venus | Orbiter |
| *Vega 1* | USSR | 1984 | 1985 | Venus | Lander and atmospheric balloons |
| Continued on to | | | 1986 | Halley's Comet | Flyby |
| *Vega 2* | USSR | 1984 | 1985 | Venus | Lander |
| Continued on to | | | 1986 | Halley's Comet | Flyby |
| *Giotto* | ESA | 1985 | 1986 | Halley's Comet | Flyby |
| *Sakigake* | Japan | 1985 | 1986 | Halley's Comet | Flyby |
| *Magellan* | USA | 1989 | 1990 | Venus | Orbiter |
| *Galileo* | USA | 1989 | 1991 | Asteroid Gaspra | Flyby |
| Continued on to | | | 1993 | Asteroid Ida | Flyby |
| Continued on to | | | 1995 | Jupiter | Orbiter, probe |
| *Ulysses* | ESA | 1990 | 1992 | Jupiter | Flyby |
| Continued on to | | | 1994–95 | Sun | Flyby |

ESA: European Space Agency

# SPACE ORGANIZATIONS

If you would like to learn more about our solar system, there are many places here on Earth that you can visit. Most big cities have planetariums and science museums that offer exciting space exploration shows and exhibits. The following institutions have special programs, exhibits, or activities of interest:

**National Air and Space Museum**
Smithsonian Institution
Washington, DC 20560
(Exhibits open to the public)

**Challenger Center for Space Science Education**
1055 North Fairfax Street
Suite 100
Alexandria, VA 22314
(Provides space exploration simulations for school groups in many cities)

**The Planetary Society**
65 North Catalina Avenue
Pasadena, CA 91106
(Organization devoted to increasing our knowledge of the solar system)

**U.S. Space Camp/Space Academy and Aviation Challenge**
U.S. Space & Rocket Center
One Tranquillity Base
Huntsville, AL 35807
(Operates Space Camps near the NASA Marshall Space Flight Center in Alabama and the NASA Kennedy Space Center in Florida)

# FOR FURTHER READING

For further information about our solar system, the following are recommended:

Asimov, Isaac. *How Did We Find Out About Pluto?* New York: Walker and Company, 1991.

Brewer, Duncan. *Planet Guides.* Volumes on: *Comets, Asteroids, and Meteorites; Jupiter; Mars; Mercury and the Sun; The Outer Planets.* Volumes on: *Uranus, Neptune, and Pluto; Planet Earth and the Universe; Saturn; Venus.* New York: Marshall Cavendish, 1992.

Cattermole, Peter. *Planetary Exploration: Mars.* New York: Facts on File, 1989.

Crump, Donald J., ed. *Exploring Your Solar System.* Washington, D.C.: National Geographic Society, 1989.

Fraser, Mary Ann. *One Giant Leap.* New York: Henry Holt, 1993.

Gallant, Roy. *National Geographic Picture Atlas of Our Universe.* Washington, D.C.: National Geographic Society, 1980.

Kelch, Joseph. *Small Worlds: Sixty Moons of Our Solar System, from Galileo to Voyager 2.* New York: Simon & Schuster, 1990.

Lauber, Patricia. *Seeing Earth from Space.* New York: Orchard Books, 1990.

Ride, Sally, and Tam O'Shaughnessy. *The Third Planet: Exploring the Earth from Space*. New York: Crown, 1994.

*Scientific American*, Special Issue on Life in the Universe, October 1994. Includes articles on: "Life in the Universe," "The Evolution of the Universe," "The Earth's Elements," "The Evolution of the Earth," "The Origin of Life on the Earth," "The Evolution of Life on the Earth," "The Search for Extraterrestrial Life," "The Emergence of Intelligence," "Will Robots Inherit the Earth?," and "Sustaining Life on the Earth."

Silver, Donald. *Earth: The Ever-Changing Planet*. New York: Random House, 1989.

Vogt, Gregory L. *Apollo and the Moon Landing* (1991); *The Hubble Space Telescope* (1992); *Magellan and the Radar Mapping of Venus* (1992); *Viking and the Mars Landing, Missions in Space* (1991); *Voyager* (1991). Brookfield, Conn.: Millbrook Press.

# INDEX